Keep Safe!

TEN THINGS YOU CAN DO RIGHT NOW TO ENHANCE YOUR SAFETY AND PROTECT YOUR FAMILY:

1. Plan an escape route from every room in your home. Make sure everyone understands exactly what it means and how it works. *(See item 2, Family Fire Drills)*

2. Put together an emergency kit for your car. Include basic tools, a flashlight, jumper cables, rope, motor oil, antifreeze/coolant, a blanket, and first aid supplies. Involve any teenage drivers in the household in the project. *(See item 21, Driving Privileges, and item 88, Equipping for Safety)*

3. Place one of your business cards in your child's backpack and athletic bag, and in the pocket of every jacket your child wears. Check for them and replace them, if necessary, on the first day of every month. *(See item 27, Carrying ID)*

4. Remind your child every day that there is nothing more precious to you than her safety and that no one has the right to hurt her in any way. *(See item 17, Setting Limits)*

5. Whenever you have a choice, choose light over dark since criminals often enhance their own chances of success by doing their work under cover of darkness. And as often as you can, ensure that you have a choice. *(See item 64, Avoiding Darkness)*

6. Establish a relationship with one or two trustworthy neighbors with the specific understanding that you or your kids can contact them in case of emergency and vice versa. *(See item 12, Looking out for Each Other)*

7. Anytime you leave work late and don't feel comfortable walking to your car, request an escort. *(See item 63, Safe Routes to Work)*

8. Ask your child if she has been educated about her school's crisis management plan or if disaster drills are conducted. If not, call the principal and request that students be trained properly. *(See item 39, Crisis-Management Plans)*

9. As you travel, keep track of mileage markers and landmarks. Should your car break down, you'll be able to communicate your location quickly. *(See item 93, Responding to Trouble)*

10. If a fire alarm sounds, evacuate. Don't ever assume the alarm is false. *(See item 98, Hotels and Motels)*

For Bob and Mary, Amy and Callie, Alden and Anne Caitlin.

Dedicated also to our parents, Papa Joe and Emile, and Jim and Marilyn, and to our mentors, Robert O. Heck and W. L. Person, Jr. and to true heroes: public safety professionals everywhere.

For more information about the authors, please consult their website, www.wellsmorris.com.

For additional *Keep Safe!* information, to learn about additional *Keep Safe!* projects, or to submit your safety tip or story, contact www.tokeepsafe.com.

ORDERING:

Trade bookstores in the U.S. and Canada please contact:
Publishers Group West
1700 Fourth Street, Berkeley CA 94710
Phone: (800) 788-3123   Fax: (510) 528-3444

Hunter House books are available at bulk discounts for textbook course adoptions; to qualifying community, healthcare, and government organizations; and for special promotions and fundraising. For details please contact:
Special Sales Department
Hunter House Inc., PO Box 2914, Alameda CA 94501-0914
Tel. (510) 865-5282   Fax (510) 865-4295
e-mail: ordering@hunterhouse.com

Individuals can view our books on the Web at **www.hunterhouse.com** and can order our books from most bookstores or by calling toll-free:
1-800-266-5592

Keep Safe!

101 WAYS TO ENHANCE YOUR SAFETY AND PROTECT YOUR FAMILY

Donna K. Wells, M.A., M.P.A.
and Bruce C. Morris, J.D.

Foreword by David Baldacci

Hunter House
PUBLISHERS

Hunter House Inc., Publishers
P.O. Box 2914
Alameda CA 94501-0914

LIBRARY OF CONGRESS CATALOGING-IN-PUBLICATION DATA:

Wells, Donna Koren, 1951-
Keep safe! : 101 ways to enhance your safety and protect your family /
Donna K. Wells & Bruce C. Morris ; foreword by David Baldacci.–1st ed.
p. cm.
Includes bibliographical references and index.
ISBN 0-89793-287-0 (HC) – ISBN 0-89793-286-2 (PB)
1. Home accidents–Prevention. 2. Safety education. I. Morris, Bruce C. II. Title
TX150 .W45   2000
613.6–dc21   00-021085
         CIP

PROJECT CREDITS:

COVER DESIGN: Graciela Galup Design   BOOK DESIGN: Brian Dittmar
EDITOR: Kelley Blewster   PROOFREADER: Susan Burckhard
PRODUCTION DIRECTOR: Virginia Fontana
ACQUISITIONS COORDINATOR: Jeanne Brondino
ASSOCIATE EDITOR: Alexandra Mummery   PUBLICITY DIRECTOR: Marisa Spatafore
CUSTOMER SERVICE MANAGER: Christina Sverdrup
ORDER FULFILLMENT: Joel Irons, A & A Quality Shipping Services
PUBLISHER: Kiran S. Rana

Printed and bound by Publishers Press, Salt Lake City, Utah
Manufactured in the United States of America

9   8   7   6   5   4   3   2   1   First Edition   00 01 02 03 04

Table of Contents

Foreword

The stretch of beach was an unfamiliar one. The surf was rough and the waves a little high. And yet the water was wonderfully refreshing under a tropical sun and there were dozens of people in the ocean. Some were body surfing, others kayaking, still others just swimming, and a few merely standing in waist-deep water catching rays. There were six in our group: my wife and I, our two children, and my in-laws. I had my three-year-old son in my arms and was in water not even up to my chest. We were jumping the waves and having a grand time. We were talking and laughing with the others, which probably was why I didn't see the very large wave that knocked me flat and ripped by son from my arms.

I staggered up, spitting saltwater and looking frantically for my boy. After a few panic-stricken seconds I saw him under me, eyes peering up in shock at his dad from three feet of water. I reached down and snatched him up before the tide might have swept him away forever. He was crying. I was too terrified to cry. I just sat there on the sand holding him. He asked me why I had let him go, and I had no answer to such a simple question. I had heard of such tragedies happening to others, but I was certain it could never happen to me. Well, it almost did. In fact it might very well have if the water hadn't been so clear, or my reflexes a bit slower, or if my son had not miraculously been in that exact spot. I still have nightmares about it: my son looking up at me and asking why I let him go.

I am a cautious man, perhaps even overprotective with my children. Sometimes, I stop my children from doing things I did as a child for fear they will be hurt. As a youngster growing up in Richmond I spent many an hour in the emergency room as the result of some daredevil activity, behavior that gave my parents sleepless nights, I'm sure. The emergency room at Richmond Memorial Hospital wasn't named after me, but it could have been, based simply on the number of stitches I received there. But I am careful now. Our home has first-rate security, fire alarms, carbon monoxide detectors, fire extinguishers, motion detectors, deadbolts, and window pins. All that stuff. I'm a careful driver, with not even a speeding ticket in the last fifteen years. I keep my eyes glued to my children when we go shopping lest someone try to take them. And yet I let a wave of water take my son from me because I wasn't aware enough. Because I wasn't careful enough.

Keep Safe! has lots of sound advice: how to prevent accidents involving yourself as well as others; how to better safeguard your home and person against violation; how to be smarter about personal safety while away from home; and ways to spot certain behavior in your children stemming from peer pressure that may lead to problems later on, to mention just a few. Many of the items are common sense, but many are not. Many are ones I would never have known, but for reading this book. You can't prevent all accidents, of course, and you can never be completely safe, but you always can be more educated and informed with respect to such matters. This guide will help you do that, and I commend Donna Wells and Bruce Morris for putting such a helpful book together. Be smart. And be safe.

DAVID BALDACCI
April 2000

Preface

I grew up in a caring, middle-class family. My father was a meat cutter, my mother a secretary. From the start, my parents sought to instill in me the same values of hard work and discipline that served them so well. They believed there was no more important duty for them as parents and as good citizens.

In my years as a prosecuting attorney, as Attorney General of Virginia, and now as Governor of the Commonwealth of Virginia, I have found that I rely on the same virtues and ideals I was taught as a child. We learn them when we are youngsters and we never outgrow them. These characteristics transcend age; they transcend activity. They rise above differences among cultures and countries, regions and religions. They are the universal attributes: responsibility, honesty, compassion, stewardship, kindness, honor, and freedom.

Each of us carries memories of times when these characteristics were exhibited to us in some memorable way. But these attributes do not come automatically. They cannot be turned on and off. It takes effort to make them part of the very fiber of a being. They require years of teaching, by instruction and by example. That's what my parents did; that's what my wife Roxane and I try to do. And that is what this book suggests.

You can take the responsibility for your safety. Not just once or twice a day. Not just when your child is small. Not just when you are afraid or unsure. But every day, in a positive, thoughtful way.

In this book, Donna and Bruce emphasize the need to *think* safe and *act* safe to *be* safe. Their premise that each of us can take active steps to enhance our safety and protect our families embodies three attributes that are essential to Americans everywhere: freedom, responsibility, and commitment.

Ours is a democratic nation—built on the ideals of individual liberty and freedom. There may be no quality more dear to this nation and its history than freedom. Freedom of thought, freedom to act within the bounds of law, freedom to choose those who will lead us, freedom to pursue our dreams and raise our families as we see fit. We are free to *think* about our own safety, rather than expecting government to do it all for us—and, perhaps, consequently having our freedoms restricted by government.

But with freedom comes personal responsibility. To act in accordance with the law. To be accountable for one's actions. To be active in our support of safety, justice, and honor. As a former state prosecutor, I appreciate the emphasis this book places on citizens becoming involved in safety. Not just the police but the entire criminal justice system needs to be supported by an informed and active citizenry.

Responsibility demands that we do all we can to act in as safe a manner as possible, reducing risks for ourselves and for others. Responsibility requires that we think before we act, and that we act with the best of intentions.

I am especially pleased that this book encourages parents to teach their children that civic responsibility is just as important as freedom. Our youngsters should learn at an early age the value of good citizenship and the necessity of looking out for one another.

If we enjoy freedom and accept the responsibility that comes with it, then we must also make a commitment to change our behaviors and to do all that we can to ensure the safety of others—to *be* safe. As a parent, I was gratified to find several practices that endorse parents' setting limits for children. I believe that is a parental responsibility that children want as much as they need.

If you make a commitment to follow the practices identified in this book, they will quickly become habits. You will drop one of your business cards in your child's jacket so that he carries identification (and your phone number) with him. You will always let someone know your travel schedule. You will become aware of highway landmarks and mile markers. You will notice lighting and traffic patterns. You will be safe and you will help others to be safe. And you will make a difference.

Yet we cannot be truly free if we live in fear of those who would use brute force to commit crimes against the law-abiding. We cannot be free if our neighbors hide behind locked doors, if our grandparents are afraid to walk through our neighborhoods, if we worry about our children's safety in schools or on our streets. We cannot be free if fear restricts our freedom of movement or opportunity.

Fear is like a disease that, left unchecked, can spread quickly, overtaking even the healthiest of communities. For years we allowed it to proliferate, until for many people it dominated their lives. Fortunately, like many diseases, fear can also be prevented by taking proactive steps to alleviate risk. This book provides a fresh approach to doing just that. Each of these habits can be adopted into daily routines and schedules. They can become just as much a part of your day as waking up or getting dressed—and just as automatic.

I have spent most of my life serving the People. Those of us in public service have no higher purpose than to govern as servants of the People, never crossing the line to where our decisions cause them to be servants of government. The People are our reason for existing and they are the first line of defense in safety.

As citizens, each of us is the master of his own destiny. That doesn't mean we can control everything that will happen to us, but it does mean we can direct much of it. That is what makes the American dream possible. And that is what makes this book so very useful.

Just as we are a people that value freedom, so, too, are we a country built on independence. We don't want government directing our lives, nor should it do so. We want to be independent—to walk where we want to walk, to travel safely, to camp or boat without fear of harm from others. We have the ability to make that happen. The government doesn't safeguard your home. You do. The government doesn't landscape your yard. The government doesn't decide when or where you work. You have the freedom to determine each of those choices in the safest manner possible.

Yes, we have a civic responsibility to keep others as safe as we can. We are fortunate that crime rates and accident rates keep falling. But I am one of those who believe that no crime rate is acceptable, that no accident should be expected. Reduction in crime is not enough. I don't want to reduce crime; I want to eliminate it. I've spent my professional life with that goal in mind.

I believe the best way to accomplish that goal is through personal action. With this book you will be well equipped to do so. And if all of us follow these practices, then your safety and my safety will build on each other. Your attitude and mine will support others. Your prevention and mine will multiply. That is what we as Americans do best—support and protect one another, through the individual proactive efforts of each of us.

Each of us has been blessed with the opportunity to live the American dream. For no one does the dream include criminal activity or accidents. Rather, the dream embraces the security of safety for ourselves and the ones we hold most dear. I hope you will take these steps to ensure that security.

JAMES S. GILMORE, III
Governor of Virginia

Acknowledgements

Someone (probably an agent) said, "No author succeeds by his efforts alone." We agree with that assertion. Our book was a collaborative effort, to be certain, and one for which we owe much to many. The information we impart with the hope of making others safer, we have gathered over decades from the knowledge and experiences of many people. The credit for our work is shared by a number of friends and colleagues who helped produce what follows. The mistakes are ours alone. We can't mention everyone here. Those to whom we are most grateful for their advice, patience, example, and encouragement are:

David Baldacci, exceptional storyteller and new friend, whose foreword, in a few words, captures the essence of our message;

Colonels M. Wayne Huggins and W. Gerald Massengill, the former and the current Superintendents of the Virginia State Police, true professionals we are honored to have as close friends;

Dr. William C. Bosher, Jr., Superintendent, Chesterfield County (Virginia) Public Schools, and former Henrico County Superintendent of Schools and Virginia State Superintendent of Schools, the best administrator we know, a good friend, and a true teacher;

G. Russell Stone, Jr. and Christine L. Turner, long-time friends, colleagues and two of the best prosecutors anywhere;

The Honorable M. Randolph Carlson, II, Judge, 4th District Juvenile and Domestic Relations Court, Commonwealth of Virginia, another long-time, close friend and fellow former prosecutor;

Richard L. Piermarini, photographer extraordinaire;

Kiran Rana, Jeanne Brondino, and all of the fine professionals at Hunter House;

and, of course, our families.

Important Note

The material in this book is intended to provide suggestions that will increase the safety of you and the people about whom you care. Every effort has been made to provide accurate and dependable information. The contents of this book have been compiled through professional research. However, professionals in the field have differing opinions and changes are always taking place, so some of the information may become outdated or impractical.

Therefore, the publisher, authors, and editors cannot be held responsible for any error, omission, professional disagreement, outdated material, or adverse outcomes that may derive from the implementation of any of the recommendations made in this book, nor can they ensure that employing these suggestions will guarantee personal safety.

Introduction

For us, two public-safety professionals who have spent our careers serving in state and local government, the pertinent question is not so much "Why did you write this book?" but rather "Why didn't you write this book sooner?" For us, the answer to that question was really a need. We have spent our professional lives reinforcing the belief that *the primary role of government is the protection of its people*. One of us (Donna) is a former high school teacher, youth/school safety specialist, and policy and planning director who now, as Assistant Secretary of Public Safety for the Commonwealth of Virginia, coordinates the Governor's school and youth safety initiatives. The other (Bruce) served two terms as a Commonwealth's Attorney, was director of the Virginia Department of Criminal Justice Services, and Chairman of the Virginia Parole Board, and now serves as Deputy Secretary of Public Safety overseeing operations for all state public safety agencies.

Over the years, our focus has evolved from the community level in Virginia Beach and Harrisonburg, Virginia, to the state level, to national public safety efforts. In that time, we've trained thousands of public-safety professionals in the criminal-justice process. We've taught and been taught, lectured and listened. With over forty years of experience between us, we've fought fires and criminals, ignorance and arrogance. While working together on a state crime prevention plan, we discovered that we shared a passion for writing and a determination to do more to make everyone safer. As authors and collaborators, we wrote *Keep Safe!* to attempt to make that happen.

As much as we are certain that ensuring citizens' safety is the first and most important role of government, we believe just as strongly in individual freedom and responsibility. We don't expect, nor do we want, any government to have complete control over the safety of our families. In fact, all our years of speaking, training, and writing about safety only reinforce our long-standing view that the first line of defense for safety lies with you and your family, your neighbors and friends, your colleagues and fellow travelers.

We don't know who lives in your neighborhood. We don't know who has a legitimate reason to be in your child's school. We don't know your colleagues at work or the people in your community. But you do.

We do know the theories, the policies, and the tenets of public safety. And we've had a good deal of experience with the criminal mind. We've taught police officers how to prevent crime and how to respond to it; we've prosecuted criminals; we've interviewed and profiled violent serious offenders. We've developed local, state, and federal plans to address crime and safety challenges. We've written legislation, policy, and handbooks. While everything we have done in our careers has been with one goal in mind—to make our communities safer for you and your family—we have been talking *about* you, instead of *to* you.

Now, with this book, you are our focus, and this is our ultimate goal: to keep you and every person—every single law-abiding individual—as safe as possible. And we have come to believe that the best way to do that is to speak directly to you. All of the criminal justice theories we have taught, all of the safety strategies we have developed, all of the programs we have put in place can be transferred into practices you can adopt to reduce your risk and increase your safety. *To be safe, you must act safe. To act safe, you must think safe. Keep Safe!* teaches you how to do just these things.

HOW TO USE THIS BOOK

Keep Safe! is an easy-to-use book of methods you can employ every single day wherever you happen to be. It is organized in an accessible, list-like format. It is proactive, focusing on specific, preventive actions rather than on fear and reactivity. Many of the practices will seem like common sense, and you'll say to yourself, "Well, I already knew that." But the operative word here is *practice*. You *know* it, but do you *do* it? We want you to learn these practices, incorporate them into your routines, and make habits of as many as you can every day and in every way possible. For example, you know it makes good sense when you travel to be aware of where you are at all times. But do you make it a *habit* to look at mile markers, exit signs, street names, and distinguishing landmarks?

We have also included many strategies we have picked up over the years that may not be so familiar to you, but that we believe will significantly reduce your risk of becoming a victim. You may not know a great deal about controlling access through environmental design, but CPTED (Crime Prevention Through Environmental Design) has been proven to reduce the opportunity for crime. There are several ways you can incorporate CPTED into your daily life.

Readers of all ages and households of all makeups will benefit from adopting—and adapting—the guidelines set forth in *Keep Safe!* The suggestions are grouped into six major topic areas based generally on the ways many of us spend our lives and occupy our time. They include: home, school, community, work, play, and travel. Within each chapter we've collected the practices that seem to have the most logical connection with the title and with each other. In the chapter on play, for example, we describe habits you may want to adopt if you use a high school track for exercise. Some of these same methods can be practiced when you are walking down a lonely road at night. Use the skills, share them, transfer them to other facets of your life. Even if you don't have children, we encourage you to support your community by learning about school safety. Protecting our children—who will shape our future—is truly a universal concern. Maybe you'll decide that participating in your school district's "safe house" program is a great way to offer community service.

Several of the strategies transcend all categories. One of them is the buddy system. There is no better way to protect yourself than to travel, play, or work with a friend or colleague—a buddy. Have your child walk to school with a buddy. Exercise with a buddy. Shop with a buddy. Walk to the office from the parking lot with a buddy. Travel with a buddy. When it comes to safety, two are nearly always better than one.

Another is awareness. Always be mindful of your surroundings. Always look for exits. Always know who else is nearby. Always make note of the time of day, of weather, and of lighting conditions. At the beginning of each chapter, we'll discuss more of these universal habits that transcend time and place.

Finally, *Keep Safe!* is designed to be applied in a variety of ways. Because we want to make it easy for you to build these practices into your everyday life, we've kept the format simple. Pick up the book even when you have only a few minutes to spare; that's all the time you need to study a handful of new methods for increasing your safety. Or you may wish to select one topic and go through it from beginning to end. If you're about to take a trip, start with the chapter on travel. Is your child riding the bus for the first time? Begin with the chapter on school. Or, if you prefer, skip around. Pick one suggestion a day or two a week. Let your youngster select the pages.

None of the suggestions require special training. Most are free or cost very little. You may decide that some will work better than others for you and your family. As with anything, take what you like and leave the rest. But we wish to emphasize that while we cannot promise that you will go through life free from harm, we do believe that if you perform these practices on a regular basis—if you and your family members make them habits—you will significantly reduce your risk of becoming a victim.

So, why did we write this book? For you and your family—and for us and ours. Be safe.

DONNA K. WELLS AND BRUCE C. MORRIS

at home

If there is anywhere we want to feel safe, need to feel safe, expect to feel safe, and have some right to feel safe, it is in our homes. We center our lives there, maintaining all that is precious to us in our place of abode. Whether we live in cabin or castle, we close the door and establish our privacy and propriety. We do so believing that what is ours is ours and that all who dwell under our roof are free from harm. Are they?

Residential burglaries remain unacceptably high. Household accidents kill thousands of Americans, all ages, all makeups, each year. Fires and natural disasters cause property damage measured annually in billions of dollars. Once nearly every minute of every day a fire hits a home, and an average of twelve people a day lose their lives due to fire and smoke in the home. Believe it: the impact on all of us from these events is measured in more than increased insurance premiums; they equate to a significant depreciation in the quality of life.

Can we do anything to prevent, deter, or reduce these statistics? You bet we can. And we all bear responsibility. The fundamentals of personal safety begin with what we practice in our homes. And with what we teach our children. Like it or not, our habits often become their habits. If they see us employing safe practices around the house and yard, they are much more likely to think safe and be safe at home and elsewhere, whether we are around or not. Awareness promotes the recognition of what must be done and the adoption of habits and routines that can save lives.

And so does example. When we lock the doors at night and turn on the outside lights, our kids are watching. Every time we buckle our seat belts (or forget to) our children see us and take notice. When we point out landmarks and make note of unusual sights, we're training them to do the same. Safety can be just as much a part of your daily routine as getting dressed in the morning and going to work or school.

So what do we do? Smoke detectors and proper locks are givens, right? In reality, crimes and accidents still occur that might have been prevented had simple, inexpensive devices been installed. Perhaps more surprising is the number of tragedies resulting when smoke detectors have dead batteries or doors are left unlocked. Merely knowing what to do or owning the right safeguards is not sufficient. Unless safety precautions are put into practice correctly, they are worthless.

Exercise good fire safety in your home.

Every year nearly five thousand Americans lose their lives due to fire and smoke. Another twenty-one thousand suffer serious injury. A house in the United States is touched by fire once every minute. Nearly 80 percent of all deaths by fire happen in homes. Children under age five are twice as likely as all other people to die by fire. The statistics go on, but most of this death, injury, and destruction can be prevented.

- Install a smoke detector on every level of your home and outside every bedroom, as well as in the attic, basement, and garage. Check the batteries monthly and replace them each fall and spring when you change your clocks.

- If you need help with proper placement and installation of your smoke detectors, call your local fire department.

Place a fire extinguisher on every floor of your home in a location everyone knows. Be sure the whole family knows how to use the apparatus and that it is replaced or recharged when depleted.

- Ensure that each second-floor bedroom has its own fire-escape ladder.

- Cook safely, keeping items that could catch fire away from stoves, ovens, and range tops.

- Use safety plugs in electrical outlets and don't overload outlets or circuits.

- Replace worn cords and avoid running them under furniture and carpet.

 Don't smoke in bed.

- Secure matches, lighters, and flammable fluids out of children's reach.

- If you have a kerosene or natural-gas space heater, don't allow your children to light it or play near it.

- Keep space heaters away from window treatments, bedding, toys, and other flammable items.

- If you have an oil or natural-gas furnace, store all flammable substances such as varnish, paint thinner, gasoline, and heating oil in a separate part of your home from the furnace.

- Assure your children that firefighters are their friends who will help in the event of an emergency.

☎ Teach your children how to call for emergency assistance.

- If you live in an apartment or a dorm, always evacuate when the fire alarm sounds. Don't ever assume that the alarm is false.

2. FAMILY FIRE DRILLS

In the event of a house fire, make sure every member of your family knows exactly what to do.

If you ask your child what to do in the event of a fire, he'll likely say, "Stop, drop, and roll." That basic response is taught during Fire Prevention Week in nearly every elementary school in the country. And with good reason. We all need to know it. But we also need to make sure that we know what else to do in the event of a house fire.

Plan an escape route from every room in your home, then sit down as a family and discuss it. Make sure everyone understands exactly what it means and how it works.

- Have someone in the family make a sketch of the route and keep it posted. Kids are usually more than willing to do this.

- Practice the route at least a couple of times a year so that it's not forgotten. Use a timer. Start in different rooms. Make it a game.

Identify a meeting spot outside (and a good distance away from) the house. Make sure everyone knows that's the first place to go to meet and check on the rest of the family.

Let everyone in the family hear the smoke detectors so they'll be familiar with the sound.

- Make sure your kids understand that in the event of fire they need to get out of the house and stay out. They must never return to look for a pet or a favorite belonging, even if the fire doesn't appear to be affecting the entire building.

3 . PREVENTING
TOXIC FUME POISONING

Guard against the potentially deadly risk of breathing toxic fumes.

This is an all too familiar story of tragedy: over the holidays a few years ago, carbon monoxide poisoning killed an entire family in a small apartment building in our city. Fortunately, several other families escaped in time. Carbon monoxide (chemical symbol: CO) is a gas produced whenever any fuel such as natural gas, oil, kerosene, wood, or charcoal is burned. Because CO is odorless and colorless, levels can build up in a home without anyone knowing it. The odor of kerosene can be detected, and it is just as dangerous.

✗ Have any fuel-burning appliances—such as a natural-gas furnace, stove, or water heater; an oil furnace; a kerosene heater; a wood-burning stove or fireplace—properly and professionally installed.

▸ Have such appliances inspected by a trained professional once a year.

▸ Choose appliances that vent their fumes to the outside whenever possible.

▸ In a room where a fuel-burning appliance is operating, crack a window to ensure enough air for ventilation (but wedge wooden dowels above the open-window's sash to keep intruders out).

⊘ Don't sleep in a room with an unvented gas or kerosene space heater.

▸ Never use a charcoal grill indoors, even in a fireplace.

▸ Buy and use a carbon monoxide detector. They are relatively inexpensive, feature an easy-to-read LED display, and can be placed in a prominent place. (But be aware that such devices are no substitute for proper installation and maintenance of your fuel-burning appliances.)

Teach your children to glance at the detector every time they walk in the room.

▸ Make sure all family members learn the early symptoms of carbon monoxide poisoning (headache, nausea, and fatigue).

▸ Be conservative—if you or a family member experiences these symptoms, don't write them off as the flu or food poisoning. Get fresh air immediately and head to an emergency room. Tell the physician you suspect carbon monoxide poisoning.

Keep the kerosene supply safely away from the heater and don't light the heater when you are using anything flammable such as varnish or paint.

4 . LANDSCAPING

Plant the right landscaping to help keep your home safe.

Ever try to walk through a row of holly bushes or a line of Colorado spruce trees? Neither did we until we began studying the principles of Crime Prevention Through Environmental Design (CPTED). CPTED teaches that what we choose to plant and where we plant it can make us safer. In fact, one of the easiest ways to keep your home burglar-proof is through landscaping. A criminal committing random crimes will always look for the easiest target. Even visual borders create psychological barriers.

Plant a row of holly bushes or other thorny shrubs as close to the front and back of your home as possible, especially directly below windows, but choose varieties that won't pose a fire hazard or grow so tall as to obstruct your view to the street or other entrances to your property. The shrubs should serve as barriers, not places of concealment.

► If you don't like fences, define the borders of your property by planting a row of trees or a flowerbed. You'll be surprised; it might even keep the neighborhood kids from using your yard as a cut-through.

☼ Direct people toward the route you want them to take by providing a sidewalk and lights that guide their way to the door or, in rural areas, by ensuring that all driveways and walking paths are well lit.

► Don't plant large, "friendly" (that is, non-thorny) bushes close to your exterior doors. They invite hiding places for someone who might want to surprise you.

5 . LOCKS

If you want to keep someone out, lock him out.

Every fall in the southeastern states, as in many other parts of the country, burglaries occur while folks are at home but outside working in the yard. The thieves, typically traveling in groups and not staying in one place very long, drive into a comfortable neighborhood and fan

out, looking for houses where the residents are raking leaves or cleaning out flower beds. One of them will ring the doorbell. If no one answers, he simply walks in, takes what he wants (usually jewelry and cash

because they can be easily secreted and carried off), and walks out. Usually, several hours pass before the homeowner knows he has been the victim of a crime.

 Ensure that each of your exterior doors and windows is equipped with an effective lock, properly installed. Doors are best secured with deadbolt locks that have at least a one-inch throw. On windows, especially on older windows, the sash lock is usually not sufficient. Consult a hardware or building supply professional to determine what type of pin or screw lock would work best with your window frames.

$\Rightarrow$

Keep your windows and doors locked, even when you're home.

► Key all of your exterior doors to the same key for convenience, key control, and rapid access in an emergency.

If you're working outside, leave only the door(s) within your line of vision unlocked.

► Be sure that windows in the bedrooms of children, the elderly, or the handicapped can be opened quickly in an emergency.

► Don't leave first-floor windows open at night. Screens only keep bugs out; they don't protect anyone.

► If you must keep a first-floor window open at night, crack it only enough for circulation, and wedge a wooden dowel above the sash to prevent its being opened further.

► Check all your windows and locks on a regular basis, to ensure they are in good working order.

When you decide to get away from it all, don't invite someone else to come in.

Thieves aren't necessarily the brightest people in the world, but they do know how to take advantage of opportunity. If you leave for a week or even for a weekend, don't advertise the fact. Making things easy for criminals makes life hard for you.

☎ Don't let your newspapers or mail pile up. Either call and have delivery temporarily stopped, or ask a neighbor to pick them up for you.

💡 Use timers on several lights inside your home. Have them set to go on and off at different times.

▸ Don't leave a message on your voice mail or answering machine indicating that you're away.

👁 Have a neighbor keep an eye on your home.

▸ If you're gone for an extended period of time, make arrangements to have the grass cut, the shrubs trimmed, and the "lived-in" look maintained.

▸ Don't put your travel dates on a wall or kitchen calendar. If a thief does get in, he'll know whether or not he can come back later for more.

💡 Keep your outside lights on or on timers or motion detectors.

▸ If possible, keep a vehicle parked in your driveway.

7. LIGHTS AND LIGHTING

Don't allow criminals to use the cover of darkness to invade your home.

Are you afraid to walk down a street at night even though you feel completely comfortable there during the day? Many of us are, and criminals know that. Obviously, they like to operate when they won't be seen or recognized. If a burglar is looking for a target, and your house is lit up like a Christmas tree while your neighbor's is completely in the dark, chances are it won't be you filing the police report.

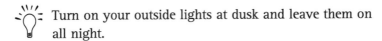 Turn on your outside lights at dusk and leave them on all night.

► If you use lighting on outdoor trees, place the light so it illuminates the area under the tree.

► Make sure the light from your outdoor lights isn't blocked by trees, fences, or walls.

► If you like to have lights shining on your home, have them aimed up and out from your foundation. Lights aimed directly at the front of your home prevent you from seeing out your windows.

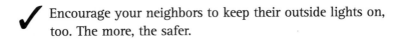 Encourage your neighbors to keep their outside lights on, too. The more, the safer.

8. MORE WAYS TO
BURGLAR-PROOF YOUR HOME

Look at your home as if you were going to try and break into it.

We know a couple of FBI agents who believe that when they are looking into the abyss, the abyss is looking back at them. We don't want you to start thinking like a career criminal, but there is real value to considering that point of view. The bad guy's perspective can be illuminating.

- Got a crawl space? It's an invitation for a bad guy. He can crawl inside, remain well-hidden, and carve his way into your home. Be sure that access doors to crawl spaces are locked.

 Follow your phone wires. Are they exposed on the exterior of your home? If so, they can easily be cut, eliminating your ability to contact help. Do what you can to keep them secure by covering exposed wires with a metal or plastic sleeve and by locking the telephone network interface device (the telephone box, usually located next to the electric meter).

- The same is true with your electricity lines. Especially in older neighborhoods, electrical wires can be easily accessed by would-be criminals. Consult your power company regarding any concern you have about the security of your power lines.

- Stand in your yard and on your street and look into your windows. Can everyone and anyone see what you're doing? If so, think about lowering your shades or blinds after sunset.

⇨

- Garage doors are another vulnerable point, especially since many of us don't lock the door leading from the garage to the house. The best garage doors, from a security standpoint, have no windows; thus, if locked, they can't be readily opened.

 Older homes that have cellars are also at risk of entry. Again, install a strong lock to control access.

9. STRANGER-PROOFING YOUR HOME

Don't automatically lower the drawbridge. Your home is your castle. It doesn't belong to strangers.

Most of us are taught to be polite—even to people we don't know; but we do not have to open our homes to them. And unfortunately, in today's society, to do so could put you and your family at risk. You can be helpful without exposing yourself to harm.

Teach your children to become aware of neighbors who are at home when you aren't. The children in our neighborhood all know who the "stay-at-home" moms are. They know to look for lights, cars, and activity at neighboring houses when they are home alone.

Always give your children strict orders never to open the door to a stranger when you aren't there. And, even more important, give them a telephone number of someone close by they can call in case the individual persists in knocking or ringing the bell. If possible, teach them an escape route (for example, out the back door to a neighbor's house).

► There are, of course, legitimate door-to-door salesmen. Unfortunately, having been trusting souls only to be stung several times, we have learned not to immediately buy items or services from strangers who show up at our doors. If you think you might be interested in the product or the cause someone is selling, ask him for literature and a phone number you can call at a later time after you make your decision.

10. TELEPHONE SAFETY

Control your phone so it doesn't control you.

How many times have you successfully pulled everyone together for a family dinner only to be interrupted by a telephone solicitation? You do not have to answer the phone every time it rings. In addition to unwanted sales calls, many scam artists or criminals may be looking for an opportunity to invade your privacy or your home. You should take advantage of technology such as caller ID to identify your callers before you answer and be careful about the information you disclose. Return calls at your convenience—or not at all.

► Immediately ask if the call is a solicitation.

► Always ask for the caller's full name, the company he represents, and the name and number of his immediate supervisor. If he can't or won't give this information to you, end the call.

Ø Never give your credit card number or social security number to someone who initiates a call to you. As quickly as law enforcement officials identify and publicize scams, the bad guys come up with new ones.

► If your caller ID indicates "unavailable" or "unknown," it is likely a commercial call. You don't have to answer it. What are you afraid you're missing?

► Many of us find it difficult to be rude, even when someone is bugging us to buy something. One suggestion is to ask the caller for his home number and tell him you will call him back at a time more convenient for you. He won't, but it will end the call.

☎ In many localities, you can call the telephone company and have "private" numbers automatically blocked.

KEEP SAFE!

11. OBSERVATION SKILLS

Train yourself and your family to be more observant.

We know a couple of investigators who are particularly successful at what they do, not necessarily because they're smarter than everyone else, but because they are more observant. For some people this talent comes naturally. Fortunately, most of the rest of us can acquire it with some concentration and practice.

Become familiar with what is usual and customary, and take notice of anything new that shows up. If you know all the cars that normally travel your street, look for odd cars parked at odd hours, or activity that doesn't fit with the environment.

- Make it a habit to always be aware of your surroundings. As you drive down a street, look for landmarks or unusual sights to help you remember where you've come from and how you got where you are.

- Study and memorize license plates, especially if you observe someone driving in an erratic or dangerous manner.

- Watch people and look for any signs that you may be entering a risky situation. If you feel like you are, leave immediately.

Teach your children the same awareness by making a game of it. See how quickly they can notice and memorize a license plate. Point out unusual sights and landmarks as you travel. See if they can identify all the owners of the cars parked on your street at any given moment. If you can make this a habit for them, you will be giving them a lifelong gift.

Be on the lookout.

Donna grew up in a small town where nearly everyone knew her; therefore, her parents almost always knew what she was doing. And if what she was doing was wrong, her parents would hear about it before she got home. She used to think that her neighbors probably didn't have much else to do. Now she knows they were, in fact, great neighbors and good friends.

► Good neighbors are invaluable. They are probably living in your neighborhood for the same reason you are: because they value it and the people in it. So help each other out, even on an informal basis.

Establish a relationship with one or two trustworthy neighbors with the specific understanding that you or your children can contact them in case of emergency and vice versa.

► If you notice something odd going on at your neighbor's house while he's at work or away, contact him. If you can't get him and you're concerned, call the police. That's what they are there for—your safety.

► Offer to pick up the newspaper or keep an eye on your neighbor's house next time she leaves town.

✔ Make a mental note of the cars that frequent your street. Get your children to do the same. Then talk about what to do when "strange" vehicles appear.

► If you and your neighbors begin to notice any vandalism or crime in your neighborhood, work together and with the police to fix it before it gets worse.

13. NEIGHBORHOOD WATCH

Whether they're informal or set up through the police department or sheriff's office, neighborhood watch programs work. Support the one in your community, or start one if one doesn't already exist.

Neighbors who know each other well and get along tend to keep an eye on the neighborhood and watch the comings and goings of traffic in the area. Over twenty years ago, when residential burglaries were skyrocketing, the National Sheriffs' Association formalized this approach, establishing the Neighborhood Watch program, which organizes individuals in particular segments of a community to look for and report suspicious or criminal activity. Whether your neighborhood's program is organized or not, such efforts work.

 Call your police department or sheriff's office if you want more information on establishing such a program.

► Use your community newsletter to help communicate safety concerns.

Establish a phone tree or street reps to alert all members of the neighborhood to particular concerns.

► Start watching your own neighborhood or street. Look for unusual activity, strange behaviors, vandalism, and neglected property. Report anything suspicious or abnormal to proper authorities.

► Invite a police officer to come to a neighborhood meeting to talk about residential crime prevention.

1 4 . CARRIER ALERT

Your postal carrier can be a lifesaver. Find out how.

Gone are the days when we believed that our safety rested solely in the hands of the police. We now recognize that safety is everyone's business. One group of people that moves through every neighborhood nearly every day of the week is postal carriers. They provide another set of eyes and ears in the community. And in many areas, the U.S. Postal Service offers an invaluable service known as "Carrier Alert," a voluntary notification program intended as a public service. They operate the program in conjunction with a local agency or organization.

✓ Each participating household registers for the program, providing an emergency contact. A decal of participation with the emergency contact info is then placed in the participant's mailbox.

▸ If a postal carrier notices that a household's mail is accumulating or notices anything else amiss on his route, he notifies the local organization. They in turn call the participant, and, if necessary, the emergency contact listed by that individual.

 If no one can be reached, local law enforcement officials are notified.

15. BACKUP TELEPHONE PLAN

Always give your children a backup telephone plan.

Every spring, Donna takes her children to the circus. They have watched the trapeze artists perform both with and without a safety net. Although it is much more exciting without the net, they usually feel better seeing the security of that net. Kids want security, too.

☎ Keep a list posted of emergency numbers (the refrigerator is a good place since it never moves or gets lost), including 911, your office, pager, and cell phone, a couple of neighbors who live nearby, a relative, and a good friend. As soon as they can, your children should be encouraged to memorize the numbers.

▸ Ask your child whom he is comfortable calling. Include that number on your emergency contact list.

⊘ Don't include any numbers that automatically ring to voice mail.

▸ Practice what to do in the event of an emergency—whom to call first under what circumstances.

👪 Consider establishing a "family emergency code" that means nothing to anyone else but will alert you if your child finds herself in a dangerous situation. For example, she can call you and say "The cat is sick," and you will know that she is at risk in some way.

▸ If you or your kids are home alone, especially overnight, keep a cell phone nearby. It provides a wonderful sense of security, especially if it has critical contact numbers preprogrammed into it.

16. KEEPING AN EYE
ON YOUR CHILD

Whether she is two or twelve, seven or seventeen, if you are legally responsible for a child, assume the obligation to know where she is and what she is doing.

One night recently, Bruce received a call from the state Emergency Operations Center (EOC) advising him of the fate of a two-year-old boy reported missing eight hours earlier. He had disappeared from his yard in one of our mountain towns. At noon when he was playing in shorts and a T-shirt, it was seventy-two degrees; by 5:00 P.M., it was twenty-eight degrees and snowing heavily. More than two hundred volunteers and professional rescue workers combed the vicinity until well after dark. Just before midnight, the little one was found less than a hundred yards from where he'd been playing, face-down in a small stream, dead. Twelve hours, forty degrees, and terrible, preventable tragedy.

Whatever her age, if you have responsibility for a child, you have the obligation to know her whereabouts at all times. She is just a child; you are the responsible adult. Honor the obligations of your role.

Even when they are very young, it only takes an instant for children to duck into the woods, disappear at the beach, or walk away at the mall. Never take your eyes off a small child in your custody. Too much can happen too fast.

▸ When they are old enough to be out in the neighborhood, you still need to know where they are and why. And they need to know that you need to know.

► If your work situation is such that you don't spend any time or just a few hours a week with your child, then consider changing your schedule. Your child is not only your responsibility, she is your first priority.

You are your child's number-one protector and cheer-leader. No one will look out for her like you should—not her teacher, not her coach, not her best friend's parent. Make sure your youngster knows that you believe in her and trust her.

► Curfews are your friend. If there is one in your town, enforce it within your household. Make sure your child knows that she can't stay out later than the curfew because she will be breaking the law and a family commitment.

► Don't ever be afraid to exercise your prerogative as a parent or guardian. You are responsible for that child. You can instill independence in your child without requiring her to act reckless-ly on her own. Let her know that the rules are there because you love her, not because you are pointlessly restricting her.

► If you use a babysitter, make sure he or she knows that family rules are to be enforced.

Give your kids one of the best gifts ever—limits.

Although we recognize the controversy behind the practice, we have been pleasantly surprised at the number of communities that have instituted youth curfews in recent years to protect, not punish, a segment of our society that is particularly vulnerable to harm and risk. That trend mirrors another national trend—the growth of teen courts,

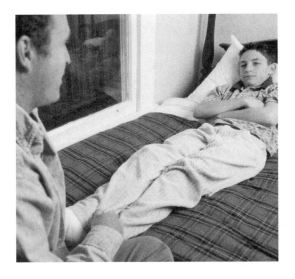

an optional but binding alternative offered to offenders whereby their own peers, other teens, hear the case and set penalties. Kids truly want limits. And they believe limits should be set for others as well. That is the theory behind teen courts, and it has made them successful.

- ▸ One of the best practices you can institute within your family is to keep each other informed of your whereabouts. Tell your kids where you will be when you leave and when they can expect you to return. Expect them to do the same.

 If your plans change, call and let them know. Expect them to do the same.

➤ If your community has a curfew, don't extend your family curfew past it. Kids need to know that you support the law and
they need to understand that they are breaking the law if they
are out past your community's curfew.

Don't ever let your kids forget that they are your most
precious "possession." Because they are so special, no one
has the right to hurt them in any way. If someone tries to, create
an environment where your children will feel free to tell you about
it immediately.

➤ Set limits on where your kids can go and with whom and stick
to those limits. It's the best way for them to internalize the need
for, and rewards of, self-discipline.

18. STAYING INVOLVED
WITH YOUR CHILD

Stay actively involved in and aware of your child's activities.

Remember the first time you had to leave your child when she was a newborn? Remember how difficult it was, how you worried about what might happen to her without you around? As our children grow older and become more independent, we must learn to let go. By the time they are teenagers, and acting like teenagers, we're often happy to get away from them for a while. But they still need us to watch out for them, to protect them, to keep them safe. A large part of meeting that obligation is being just as aware of their surroundings as when they were newborns.

- ► Your child carries much of her life to school in her bookbag each day. Do you know what's in there? Set an expectation that the bookbag will be cleaned out regularly—once a week for elementary students, twice a month for high school kids.

- ► If you have concerns about what might be in your child's purse, book bag, or gym bag, ask him or her to clean it out in your presence.

✓ If your child drives her own car, drive it yourself once a week. First, it will give you a chance to check its maintenance. Second, you can see what kinds of things are being carried around in it.

➤ Know how your child is using her computer. There is an over-whelming amount of information available on the Internet, some of it inappropriate for children. Learn what your child is accessing. You can pull down the most recent URL sites your youngster has accessed. Check them once a week to see what your child has "surfed."

Television is more violent than it used to be. It is also more available than a generation ago. Whether your child is three or thirteen, monitor what she is watching. If you don't like it, don't allow it.

➤ The same rules apply for music and films.

➤ Video games are of particular concern because they are interac-tive and many of them promote and reward violence. Be espe-cially careful of what video games your child is playing. If you don't like them, don't allow them.

We both have families with two working parents. We know how difficult it can be to monitor after-school activities and associations. But make every attempt to do so. And establish the reality that only acceptable activities will be allowed.

19. CURBING THE IMPACT OF MEDIA VIOLENCE

Don't close your eyes to the violence around you.

Whether we like it or not, our children are surrounded each day by violence. In the newspapers, on television, on the radio—wherever they go they'll read about it, see it, or hear it. The challenge is to make sure that we protect our children from adopting that violent culture as their own. The balance and perspective you instill are vital to proper value development.

- Listen to your child's language. If he uses violent language, discuss it with him at once. Don't use such language yourself, and don't allow him to do so.

- Listen to his friends. If they act or sound violent, consider prohibiting him from being with them. He may argue, but you are protecting him from a negative influence.

- Watch for any violent behavior exhibited by your child. Irrational anger, fighting, cruelty to animals, excessive teasing, and fire-setting are all early indicators of serious problems.

20. LIMITS TO PRIVACY

Maintain control and oversight of your child's room.

We believe in giving our children the privacy they need and deserve. Some experts disagree with our approach, but our children know that their privacy is not guaranteed or without limits.

Whether you live in an apartment, a condominium, or a house, you are responsible for what goes on within your "four walls," including what happens in the rooms of your children. You need to have a general idea of the activities your children are engaged in, wherever they are—bedroom, attic, garage, or basement.

 Let your child know that his room is still part of your home and that you have every right to be there.

▸ Set an example with your bedroom. Does your child feel welcome there? If so, you can set the expectation that you should feel welcome in his.

Make it a habit to go into his room at least once every day. If you see it every day, you'll be more likely to notice any changes.

▸ Look closely at his room (including the closet), the garage, the basement, the playroom, and the attic at least once a week. You don't have to snoop, just look for anything that might concern you.

21. DRIVING PRIVILEGES

Stress that driving is a privilege, not a right. It's also a tremendous responsibility.

When Donna's daughter turned sixteen, she was highly upset that her driver's education class didn't end until the week following her birthday. She expressed her disappointment to her instructor. It gave him an opportunity, and he used it, reminding her that no one automatically has the *right* to drive and that she ought to be more concerned about learning how to drive safely than about getting behind the wheel quickly.

- The minimum driving age varies from state to state, but generally, all states are becoming far more cautious about teenage drivers. If you have an aspiring young driver, call your division of motor vehicles and ask that they send you information on laws in your state that apply to teenage drivers.

Teach your child how to change a flat tire, add air to tires, check the oil, check the belts and hoses for wear, add water to the radiator, and perform other routine maintenance.

- Make sure your child understands exactly what to do in case of an emergency or an accident.

When your child gets her license, consider giving her a cell phone. Impress on her that it only be used for emergencies and only when the car is not in motion.

- With your teenager, put together an emergency kit to keep in the car. Include some tools, a flashlight, jumper cables, rope, extra motor oil and antifreeze/coolant, a blanket, and first aid supplies.

22. FAMILY DRIVING RULES

There are state driving laws and there are family driving rules—enforce both.

Motor vehicle crashes remain the number one killer of teenagers. Donna's daughter is only nineteen, yet auto accidents have already killed two of her schoolmates and made one of her childhood friends a quadriplegic—he was riding in a car with a new driver.

🚫 Remember, your child is watching (and probably modeling) you. When you are driving, don't apply makeup, read the paper, fiddle with controls, or do anything else that takes your attention from the road.

- Many states allow parents to legally revoke the licenses of their children. If you have any concerns about your child's driving ability, call and have his license revoked. Although you may incur his wrath, such a consequence is far better than his injuring himself or someone else.

- Make your family rules known up front. If Donna's child causes a crash, she loses driving privileges. If she wrecks her car, she pays for it and she doesn't get another.

- Make sure that your child understands that you allow a certain amount of flexibility for circumstances beyond his control. You don't want him to get a speeding ticket or risk his life because he's racing to get home before his curfew.

- Set limits on new drivers. Limit the hours your child can drive (e.g., only during daylight), the number of passengers allowed (e.g., only one), and where she can drive.

23. FAMILY RULES ON WEAPONS

Set family rules on weapons and make sure your child adheres to them.

The rash of school shootings in this country has reignited the argument over weapons. Who should possess them? Who should have access to them? What should be outlawed? What happens when a kid carries a Swiss Army knife to school and gets expelled? Recently, a five-year-old child in a nearby community was suspended for carry-

ing a cap gun to school. Some say the "zero tolerance" policy for weapons in schools is being carried to extremes. Other folks believe we have not gone far enough. This isn't just a school and community problem; it's a family problem.

We doubt everyone will ever agree on a weapons policy or its implementation, but our point is that you and your child should be aware of your rules, the laws in your state and community, and your school district's policy.

If you disagree with the school's rules, you can try to change them, or you can send your child to a private school with a policy more to your liking, but if your youngster remains in the school, it's your responsibility as a parent to make sure your child is adhering to the rules.

FAMILY RULES ON WEAPONS CONTINUED...

If that means no cap guns, then don't let him carry a cap gun. If it means no Swiss Army knives, then he keeps his off school property. We simply don't buy the argument that it is not a parent's responsibility to enforce school rules. For your child's safety, for the safety of others, and for your protection, know what your child has available to him. Set and enforce definite limits.

▸ Know what weapons are within your child's access. Know where they are stored and discuss with him the circumstances under which he is allowed to use them.

 Keep firearms locked up, out of sight, out of reach.

▸ Find out the specifics of your school's policy on weapons. You can call the superintendent's office, the principal, or the guidance counselor, then discuss it in detail with your child.

▸ Explain to your child that it is his civic duty to help keep his school and his community safe.

▸ Encourage your youngster to talk to you about anyone he knows who might be carrying a knife or gun, whether it's out of ignorance, fear, or a more sinister reason. Let him know he is not being a snitch; he is simply watching out for the safety of others.

☎ If you hear anything about another student that concerns you, contact his parents at once. If you believe there is a real safety threat, notify the school or police at once.

24. HOME SAFETY CHECKLIST

Plan for, prepare for, and guard against all threats to home safety—build a checklist.

Threats to your family's safety can take many forms, seen and unseen, common and uncommon. Guarding against intrusion, theft, and fire simply makes good sense, and most of us think about these things. There are some less obvious considerations that should be added to your checklist—a "work in progress" you consult and edit regularly.

✓ Have your home tested for radon.

► Set your water-heater temperature no higher than 120 degrees Fahrenheit to prevent burns.

🔓 Ensure that all guns, weapons, dangerous tools, and appliances are stored safely and locked away from children.

► Protect against injuries from falls by checking for objects that may cause trips, such as loose rugs and wobbly railings.

► Store medicines, cleaners, pesticides, paint products, and other poisons out of the reach of children.

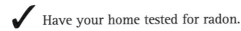 Ensure that all members of your household know basic first aid, including CPR and the Heimlich maneuver. Consider enrolling the entire family in a first aid or CPR course.

in school

S chool is the public institution many of us trust the most. It's where we spent our childhood. Now those of us who are parents send our children there several hours a day, five days a week.

At the beginning of each academic year, we leave our most precious loved ones with virtual strangers who spend more time with them than we do. Unless we choose a home-schooling option, and most of us don't, we are required by law to turn our children over to the care and custody of persons we may not have even met and about whom we know very little. We believe we need to do so in order to ensure for them the best future possible. And we hope against hope that we're doing the right thing.

It's not that we're naive. We don't always expect the best education. We know that some teachers are more effective than others. Certain schools do a better job of educating than others. But if nothing else, until fairly recently the schoolhouse has been a sheltered harbor. Our children were safe there.

Remember the first day you sent your child off to kindergarten? For many parents and children alike, it's at least a disquieting moment. Was it for you? For each of us as parents, it was a sickening feeling that lasted every minute of every hour until each child arrived safely home. Between the two of us, we have four children, ranging in age from seven to nineteen. That opening-day experience was no easier with the last child than it was with the first. In each case, we waited anxiously for the end of that interminable first day.

And how safe did *you* feel at school? When you were a kid, was there anyone who scared you? In a recent national survey, 88 percent of the parents surveyed believed that an act of violence resulting in death was possible in their school district. The rash of schoolyard killings is new, but some of the suspected causes are not. Many practitioners, including us, believe that one of the greatest indicators of tragic violence is bullying that begins with the torment, teasing, and vicious ridicule sometimes shocking to us adults. Too often recently, the persecuted have become the persecutors, inflicting hurt and injury in revengeful rage, leading to horrific events such as those in Pearl, Paducah, Jonesboro, Edinboro, Springfield, and Littleton. We react in disbelief. Perhaps our denial is a natural reaction when confronted with people's inhumanity to each other. Maybe it is born of helplessness and frustration.

What can be done? Where is intervention possible and effective? Who should be watching and what should they be reporting? How much is too much and who bears responsibility? We don't believe it takes a village to raise a child, but we acknowledge that it is naive to think every family has all the resources it requires for the task. The truth is, most families, even the most balanced and ideal, can use some help from time to time.

All of us who care—and you need not be a parent to care; we were all children once—have a role, if not a duty. We cannot do everything. Individually, we cannot save every dysfunctional family. Nor can we remove guns from every home in America. Even collectively, we lack the capacity to emotionally heal every disturbed child or repair every broken family. But each of us can make a significant difference.

We have the responsibility to protect the youngsters who are our hope for the future and to teach them to arm themselves—not with violence and weapons, but with the wisdom that comes from knowledge and experience, and with the confidence of knowing that we are doing everything we can to keep them safe and secure.

25. RIDING THE BUS

Make it your business to know about the school bus.

Ask any veteran school-bus driver: take forty or fifty students and confine them with one adult, even if it's just for a few minutes, and the potential exists for problems. There are multiple kids in each seat, large bookbags, no seat belts, and windows that can easily be opened. It is easy for parents to feel their children are particularly vulnerable when they're on the school bus.

☎ At the beginning of the school year, call the district's transportation director. He should be able to tell you the name of your child's bus driver, how many children are on the bus, and what the route will be.

► Ingrain traffic-safety rules in your child so that his actions when entering and exiting the bus are safe and become routine.

► Greet the bus driver by name and teach your youngster to do the same.

► Voice your concerns about bus safety. Ask how many students sit in each seat, how the driver controls bookbags in the aisles, and anything else that might distress or endanger your child.

 Teach your child what is and isn't acceptable behavior on a bus.

► At the end of the day, when you talk to your child about school, don't forget to ask about the bus ride.

► Get in your car occasionally and follow the bus on its route. If what you see alarms you, talk to your child and the bus driver. If you're not satisfied, involve the driver's superiors until you get the response you want. If, on the other hand, you like what you see, make it a point to commend your child and the driver.

26. WALKING TO SCHOOL

You can't keep your child in your line of vision every moment, but you should teach him what to do when he's not.

We are fortunate to live in a region served by outstanding police departments. One of the reasons the agencies are so good is that they are proactive. Another is because they listen to, and take seriously, the concerns of residents. There have been instances in the last couple of years when students walking to school were approached by strange men. The children let adults know, and the police increased their patrols in the area, located the men, and made an appropriate arrest.

When you can't be there, do all you can to promote and support backup systems, and create an atmosphere that encourages your child to talk about threats to her safety.

If your child walks to school, find a buddy for him so they can make the trip together.

► Walk with your youngster and his buddy on the first day and point out landmarks, familiar people, and traffic patterns.

► Teach them to make a game out of noting license plates and car models.

► Teach them to be aware of the route—which cars are normally parked where, which homes are usually occupied, and so on.

Make sure they know what to do in the event they are followed or approached, feel threatened, or otherwise are in harm's way.

► If your school district doesn't have a "safe house" program—where volunteer households and businesses post easily recognizable signs in their windows indicating that they are a refuge for youngsters in case of emergency—work to institute one. Make sure your child is aware of the "safe houses" located on his route to school and home.

27. CARRYING I.D.

Have your child carry identification with her at all times.

Think about your youngster at this very moment. Does she have anything on her person that provides her name and some way to contact you? Most kids, especially those in elementary school, do not. In the event of an accident or some other emergency that endangers or incapacitates your child, you will want to be contacted immediately. Take steps to ensure that will happen.

► Use labels on your child's clothing. You can order them preprinted with just about any information you wish. You don't have to sew or iron them onto everything. Instead, attach them only to her shirts or all her pants and dresses. Use a laundry pen to write your telephone number on the inside of all her shoes.

✓ Put one of your business cards in your child's backpack, athletic bag, and in the pocket of every jacket she wears. Check for and replace them on the first day of each month.

► Use a permanent marker or engraving tool to write your phone number on her bike, skates, and other equipment.

► Make sure whatever phone number you use is the one at which you can most readily be reached. It may be necessary to list two.

28. EMERGENCY CONTACT

Make sure your child has someone other than you he can go to in case of an emergency or crisis.

When Donna was a freshman in high school, a childhood friend of hers was sexually harassed by a male teacher. The girl wasn't close to her parents, so the only people she talked to were a couple of her close friends. Sadly for her, they were as ignorant of what to do as she was. In retrospect, Donna realizes they should have told someone. What the girl needed, and what her young friends did not provide, was a trusted adult to hear her story and initiate appropriate action.

▸ Find out from the school principal if your school has a school resource officer within the local police department. If so, go meet her. Talk to her about her major duties, her role as she sees it, and whether she knows or has met your child.

Whenever you get the chance, talk to your youngster about his friends and about other adults in his life. Find out if there is anyone else he can, or should, trust—a school resource officer, a coach, a school counselor, a parent with a good head on her shoulders. At some point, he or his friends may need a cooler head to prevail. Help guide him on who that should be if it isn't or can't be you.

▸ Meet and get to know your child's guidance counselor and teachers. Ask other adults whose judgment you trust about them.

29. FOLLOWING SCHOOL RULES

Ensure that your child knows the rules and that the rules are consistently enforced.

We can imagine what the evening is like for you after your child's first day of school every year. Like each of us, you probably sit at the kitchen table, reading rules and filling out forms that are to be returned to school by your child the next day. One of those forms may well be a pledge that you have seen and reviewed your school's student code of conduct. Most school districts use them. Usually, the codes are discussed with students during the first few days of school.

▸ Typically, a student code of conduct identifies school policies, including what is and is not acceptable behavior and what the sanctions will be for violations. Make sure your child understands the policies and the consequences.

✓ Take the time to read the code of conduct carefully. If there is anything with which you disagree, call the principal or superintendent and discuss it. If you aren't satisfied, call your school-board representative.

Ensure that your child understands that you expect him to live by the rules set forth.

▸ Emphasize those rules that particularly pertain to his personality, age, or situation. If your daughter likes to wear halter tops, for example, and they aren't allowed, it's your responsibility to prohibit her from wearing them to school.

30. ADDRESSING PEER PRESSURE

Acknowledge that peer pressure is a fact of life, but don't let it rule your child or your family.

How many times have you heard, "But Jamie's mother lets her do it"? To which you respond, "You are not Jamie and I am not her mother." Peer pressure is a powerful commodity. At times it can make your youngster seem like a stranger. The good news is that at some point kids learn to handle it—and it can be positive. The bad news is that they often must learn by experience—which means their families must live through it, too.

 Be proactive—steer your child to activities and individuals that are healthy and safe.

▸ There's a lot of truth to the old adage "Busy hands are happy hands." Keep your child focused by keeping him involved in organized, positive activities: sports, clubs, the newspaper, or the yearbook.

✓ Get to know your child's friends—every one of them.

▸ Get to know as many of their parents as you can. If you don't approve of what you see, talk with your child honestly about the situation and your desire to keep him safe.

▸ Take advantage of opportunities. If you watch a television program together that illustrates the negative power of peer pressure, take the time to talk with your child about it.

▸ If you have concerns about associations your child makes at school, church, or in sports, talk to the adult in charge and get her input, then discuss the situation with your youngster.

31. SCHOOL SECURITY PROCEDURES

Be sure your child's school follows visitor procedures and that staff members know at all times who is in the building.

As long as Bruce had worked in criminal justice and as much as he had advocated clear school-safety measures, he was still taken aback the first time he had to sign in at his daughter's elementary school. But it is a necessary and valuable practice.

▸ Daily attendance checks tell administrators which students are in, or absent from, school. It's equally important to know what adults are in the building and their purpose for being there.

✓ At the beginning of the school year, visit the school and note the visitor procedures. Are they clearly posted? Are they enforced? Are passes or badges disseminated to visitors, and are they collected before the visitors depart?

👁 If you volunteer in the school and know most of the personnel, keep an eye out for other visitors. Principals appreciate all the help they can get in keeping the site safe.

32. HELPING TO END BULLYING

Don't let your child be bullied.

Over the years we've talked to thousands of people about school safety. We often begin our presentations with the same question to participants: "Can you still name the bully from your childhood?" It doesn't matter if we are talking to police officers, other criminal-justice professionals, community leaders, or parents, the answer is nearly always yes. In all the years we've been doing this, only a handful of people do not remember who that person was. Bullies are seldom forgotten. We've come to believe they pose one of the biggest threats to school safety, in large part because the kids they torment can retaliate in horrific ways.

According to the National Association of Secondary School Principals, one in ten students has reported being harassed by bullies. If kids know who the bullies are (and they do), then most often school officials do too. It is your responsibility to find out if your child is being bothered or harmed in any way by a bully. But your responsibility doesn't end there. If you become aware of a problem, share that information with school or police officials.

Talk with your child regularly about his interactions with other students.

- If bullying or aggressive behavior is a problem, meet with the teacher, guidance counselor, or principal.

If several students are engaging in aggressive behavior, or a gang or clique is involved and the behavior is significant or appears to be organized, consider talking to a school resource officer or other police official.

- Be aware of bullying behavior on the bus and in the neighborhood, as well as in school.

- If your child has a persistent problem with one particular student, talk to that child's parents.

33 . SCHOOL RESTROOMS

Work with school officials to ensure that school restrooms are maintained in a way that enhances the safety and security of students.

A child we interviewed a couple of years ago displayed a behavior that is more common than most of us realize. At the end of the school day, she would rush off the bus and into the bathroom in her home. When her mother noticed the pattern and asked her about it, she found out that her daughter was afraid of the bathroom because of a group of girls who tended to frequent it. They would taunt and mercilessly tease this girl and others. Nearly every state and national school-safety survey indicates that school restrooms can be a source of fear and concern on the part of students.

✔ Walk through your child's school and locate every restroom. They should not be located under stairwells, at the end of long hallways, or in any other isolated area.

► Encourage your child to use only those that are safely located.

► The safest entrance to a restroom is not a conventional door (which typically can be locked, has no windows, and blocks sound), but rather incorporates what's known as a maze entrance. A maze entrance prohibits a line of sight into the restroom but does not obstruct sound or exit.

- Restrooms should be patrolled by adults (administrators, teachers, or parent volunteers) on a consistent basis. The exact time of the patrols should vary.

☎ Check out restroom designs and procedures at your school and voice any concerns to school staff. If you do not receive a satisfactory response, see your superintendent or school-board representative.

34. GYMNASIUMS, CAFETERIAS, AND AUDITORIUMS

Behavior expectations in school cafeterias, gymnasiums, and auditoriums should be clear and consistent, both for students and visitors.

Remember food fights in the cafeteria? They still occur. It's a fact of student life: most children believe there is one set of rules for classrooms and another for cafeterias, gymnasiums, and auditoriums. Any time there are large groups of students gathered in a less formal manner, the risk for unacceptable behavior increases. Rules and responses must be appropriate for the circumstances.

- ► It's a balancing act to let kids enjoy themselves without permitting the situation to get out of hand. Make sure you attend at least one function at your child's auditorium, library, or gymnasium at the beginning of each school year. Observe what kind of behavior is allowed. If you have concerns, call the principal at once.

58

GYMNASIUMS, CAFETERIAS,
AND AUDITORIUMS CONTINUED...

Set clear expectations with your child about her behavior in each of these areas. Make sure you aren't the parent receiving the call from the principal identifying your student as the instigator of the latest disruption.

- Take the time to walk through the gym, cafeteria, auditorium, and library with your child. Point out to her the exits, the fire alarm and extinguisher, windows, and any phones that are available.

- Volunteer to spend a lunch period in the cafeteria at least once a month and observe the students, including yours. Then talk to your child about anything you believe she needs to change.

Anytime you are in the gym, auditorium, or cafeteria, watch students as they leave to make sure you're comfortable with their exit habits in general.

KEEP SAFE!

3 5 . S T A D I U M S A N D S P O R T I N G E V E N T S

Stadiums and sports arenas, whether on campus or off, are part of school property and should be subject to the same policies as the rest of the school.

It's sometimes amazing to observe the behavior of adults at sporting events. No wonder kids adopt similar behaviors. Kids watching sports tend to get caught up in the emotions of the moment, which can cloud their judgment. The number of adults (who can keep their own feelings in check) present at any stadium function must be sufficient to control an enthusiastic, youthful crowd. A friendly police presence is especially welcome.

▸ School spirit is in fashion again, especially at sporting events. Policies that promote such spirit while disallowing any behavior that harms another student or school must be clearly established.

At the beginning of any sports season, talk with your youngster about crowds, group dynamics, the potential for mob psychology, and the effects these might have on his judgment.

▸ Go to as many games as possible—both at home and away—and watch the behavior of students. Talk to your child about any problems you observe.

If you see large numbers of students pushing or shoving each other, let a school administrator or law enforcement officer know at once in order to prevent a larger problem.

▸ If you observe that kids are allowed to jump on bleachers in large numbers, talk with the principal about the danger of such behavior.

36. SCHOOL PARKING POLICIES

Work with your school to ensure that school parking policies are enforced to maintain order during the morning and afternoon rush of students.

There are eighteen hundred students in Donna's daughter's high school and only six hundred student parking spaces. There is no more coveted prize to be obtained during the first week of school than a permanent parking decal. Conversely, there are few academic sanctions more dreaded than the loss of parking privileges.

✓ Go to your school's parking lot at least a couple of times each year to observe the opening and closing hours of school. Look for any blind spots, pedestrian risks, or potentials for mixed traffic. Call the principal if you note anything amiss.

► Even in the busiest of times, parking lots and driveways for elementary and middle schools are far more tranquil places than high school parking lots; still, open lanes should be clearly marked with arrows and lines delineating boundaries.

► Parking spaces in all school lots should be clearly identified and enforced.

► Bus traffic should be kept away from pedestrian traffic at all times.

► Student crossings should be clearly marked and manned by school personnel or volunteers at the beginning and end of the school day.

☎ If you notice that speeds are not posted or followed, notify the principal.

37. FIELD TRIPS

Enforce safety rules on field trips to ensure enjoyment and prevent disaster.

No matter what age, kids look forward to field trips. Every year, our high school band and chorus groups take field trips lasting several days and covering hundreds of miles. The parents and teachers who agree to accompany the students are very special people. The same is true for parents who agree to accompany first graders to the zoo or fourth graders to the state capitol. The chaperones' jobs will be much easier if the rules are understood in advance and enforced consistently throughout the trip.

▸ Release forms should be distributed, signed, and returned with parent and student acknowledgment of terms, conditions, waivers, and rules of conduct.

 Loading kids onto buses for a day or overnight trip is a challenge. Make sure the group has and uses a buddy system (even high school students).

⇨

► Make sure that one parent or teacher is in charge of each bus.

► Make sure there is a list of kids on each bus and that each chaperone is responsible for an identified group of students.

✔ Check to make sure that every child has the name, address, and telephone number of the school on his person.

► If possible, have all the kids wear some identifying article of clothing so they are easy to spot in a park, museum, auditorium, or other public place.

► If there are multiple buses or cars, make sure they can communicate with one another.

► Do not allow any child to remain on a bus unattended for any reason.

38. ENVIRONMENTAL DESIGN

Prevent crime in schools through environmental design.

Every day we send hundreds or thousands of students into one building for six or seven hours straight, often without a law enforcement presence. The design of that environment must enhance the safety of the students. Crime Prevention Through Environmental Design (CPTED) practices can be used in the design of schools, but they can also be used to make changes to existing structures to increase protective features.

▸ The boundaries of the school property should be clearly delineated and "No Trespassing" signs posted prominently. Legitimate users of the property should feel comfortable, but those who do not belong should know when they have crossed over onto the property and are breaking the law.

Parking lots should be designed so pedestrian traffic does not cross near bus traffic, and whenever possible, bus traffic should be kept separate from other vehicular traffic. Visitor parking should be clearly designated.

▸ Parking decals should be used.

▸ The door through which visitors can enter should be clearly marked and situated near the front office in order to ensure identification of all visitors.

▸ Halls should be monitored through closed-circuit television or through the use of volunteers.

All hallways, stairwells, locker rooms, and specialty centers should be well-lighted and as open as possible to increase safety and security.

39. CRISIS-MANAGEMENT PLANS

Crisis-management plans for schools must be in place to avert tragedy in the event of a tornado, hurricane, fire, or criminal activity.

Most of our kids have learned to "stop, drop, and roll" in the event of a fire, but we don't teach them to "lock it and block it to stop it" if they need to secure their classroom. The rash of shootings at schools across the country has heightened everyone's sensitivity to violence. A middle school near us averted tragedy from a serious weapon incident recently because officials had in place, and employed, an up-to-date crisis-management plan.

☎ Call your principal now and find out if your child's school has a crisis management plan in place. Ask how old it is, if and when the staff was trained on it, and if police and fire officials are part of the plan. Also find out if it covers medical and criminal emergencies as well as natural disasters.

✓ Check to see whether your student's school is equipped with two-way intercoms or telephones in the classrooms so teachers can contact the office in the event of an emergency in or near the classroom.

► Request that your parent-teacher organization or association help publicize the policies of the school with regard to crises.

► Ask your child if she has been educated about the school's crisis management plan or if disaster drills are conducted. If not, call the principal and request that students be trained properly.

40. SAFETY
AND SECURITY ASSESSMENTS

Schools should conduct safety and security assessments on an annual basis.

The safety of a particular school depends on many factors, including the neighborhood in which it is located, the demographics of the students who attend it, the level of parental involvement, and the history of criminal activity around it. Often a community's crime and safety problems are mirrored in its schools. Some states have begun requiring that safety and security assessments be conducted on a regular basis. It's a good idea worth your support.

☎ Call your superintendent or principal to find out if such assessments are used in your community.

► Find out if crime data from the neighborhoods surrounding the school are provided to school officials.

 As you walk through the school, look for security risks or factors that enhance safety. For example, classroom windows that are covered with construction paper or art work hinder the ability to observe activity taking place outside; however, in areas closely bordering public walkways or streets, providing optional window covering may prevent unwanted scrutiny from the outside.

► Ask your child if there is any place he feels unsafe or fearful. If so, request that the principal examine it and report back to you.

► Find out if any changes in policies or procedures have occurred as a result of safety concerns.

41. ACADEMIC EXCELLENCE

Promote academic excellence in your child to encourage self-discipline and self-esteem.

Juvenile offenders often exhibit poor academic performance. During the many years Bruce spent in juvenile courts as a prosecutor, he rarely encountered a delinquent child or young criminal with a record of excellence in the classroom.

One of the ways you can help your child develop a positive outlook and a strong character—both of which will help in times of stress or crisis—is by working with him to develop academic excellence and success.

► Expect the best academic work from your student.

► Teach him the value of solid, consistent study habits.

Work with your young child every day on schoolwork, even if it's just for a few minutes.

► If you have an adolescent, make sure he works on homework himself.

Talk with your youngster about his classes every day. Make sure you know what tests are coming up, what papers are due, and what assignments should be completed.

✓ If he is experiencing academic problems, make an appointment with his teacher, counselor, or principal to find out what the problem is. Then, together, devise a plan to solve it.

42. YOUTH SAFETY ADVISORY BOARD

If your community doesn't have a youth safety advisory board (and most do not), start one.

At last many communities grappling with youth-violence issues have begun to solicit input from their youth. Unfortunately, some communities still do not take advantage of this valuable source of information and input. We hope to see that change, and the sooner the better!

- ► While adults know a lot about what is going on in the community and in school, kids bring a different and essential point of view to any discussion. That view needs to be heard.

Call your chief of police or sheriff and ask whether he regularly receives input from the teenagers in your community. If he doesn't, suggest that he form a youth advisory board for that purpose.

- ► The board should be comprised of kids who are "doing it right" so that law enforcement officials can identify what works.

- ► In addition, citizens, parents, and local officials need to keep tabs on kids who are having problems. Those kids can provide valuable insight as to what else might be done to save or keep safe the youth in a community.

43. LAW-RELATED EDUCATION

Help make sure the teenagers in your town know and understand the laws that pertain to them.

Five years ago, we were involved in the planning and development of a statewide "law-related education" program designed to reach every middle and high school student in the state. The kids knew relatively little about the laws that applied to them and the consequences they faced. Perhaps more surprising, many parents and teachers were nearly as ignorant. Much can be gained by modernizing the civics class many of us had in high school years ago.

- There is an entire group of laws, known as status offenses, that applies to juveniles solely because of their age. If your teen or preteen doesn't know these exist, take a trip to the library with her to find out more.

✓ Check with your school to see if any law-related education (LRE) classes are taught. If not, contact your police department or the clerk of your juvenile court and request that one be offered.

- Other laws, with significant penalties, exist that pertain to everyone but that are often broken by juveniles (e.g., reckless driving, possession of a controlled substance, petit larceny). Find out if the kids in your community are taught about these laws and their consequences. If not, talk to your principal, police chief, sheriff, or juvenile authorities about getting classes in the schools.

Make sure your child understands that ignorance is no excuse. Set the example. You might even have fun learning together.

44. TEEN COURTS

Work to establish teen courts as an alternative to traditional court in your locality.

Teenagers are at high risk for committing crimes, but they are also far harder on one another than adults usually are. We have worked with troubled young people for many years, been in and out of thousands of juvenile courts and detention facilities, and have seen some approaches that work and many that don't. Teen courts have mushroomed across the nation in the last decade because in many jurisdictions they *do* work. These programs (which may require legislative action) are voluntary but binding, and are offered to juvenile offenders as an alternative to traditional court. Surprisingly, kids are usually much harder in imposing penalties on one another than are some adult judges.

- Check with your local juvenile court to determine whether a teen-court program is offered.

- If such a program is not available, pay a visit to your juvenile-court judge and talk with her about it. These judges are usually thrilled to talk with a parent whose child is not before the court.

☎ Ask the court to research whether other courts in the state have initiated such a program. If so, try to visit one.

- Find out whether your juvenile court is interested in such an alternative program. Check with your police department or local prosecutor to assess interest in the effort.

- Get to know your state legislators. If legislation is required, you will need to work with them.

in your
community

D o you feel safe in your community? As you drive, walk, shop, and move about, do you enjoy the peace of mind that comes from knowing you are in a secure environment? If not, why not? And what are you doing about it? Have you accepted some responsibility for ensuring the quality of life where you live, and are you taking action personally? Or do you feel that safety is the duty of others—primarily law enforcement officials?

The primary obligation of government is to provide for the safety of its citizens; however, we private citizens are not relieved of personal responsibility for maintaining a secure environment. A much safer community will result when we begin to work together. The purpose of this book is to aid you in doing your part to achieve just that.

According to an old story, in 1885 the World Championship Mule Team Competition was held in Chicago. The winning team pulled nine thousand pounds. The second-place team pulled slightly less. Then someone asked, "What would happen if the two teams were to pull together?" To everyone's amazement, the two teams together pulled nearly thirty thousand pounds.

As family members struggle through our busy days, we may forget to consider how much easier certain tasks are when we help each other. The same is true when it comes to promoting safety. More than a decade ago, two criminal-justice researchers, James Q. Wilson and George L. Kelling, published an article in the *Atlantic Monthly* titled "Making Neighborhoods Safe." The authors argued that if nuisance problems such as broken windows, abandoned cars, and litter are not attended to, the neighborhood deteriorates, creating an environment that invites bigger, more serious criminal activity.

The "broken windows" philosophy is not very different from the way many of us maintain our homes. Like many families, each of our households operates on a "clean as you go" approach. If someone builds a project in the basement, he is responsible for putting away the tools he uses and getting rid of trash he creates. Each family member knows dirty clothes go in the laundry room, not on the bedroom floor. Similarly, few of us allow broken windows to remain in our homes or keep junk cars and refuse in our yards. We don't let grass and weeds grow out of control or stand by as shutters and siding weather and rot.

But who paints a rented house? Who maintains property that appears to be abandoned and creates an eyesore in the neighborhood? Who bears the responsibility for alerting owners and government officials to conditions that begin as blemishes and nuisances but may grow into blight and deathtraps?

Throughout this book, you will see references to the "broken windows" approach. We're strong advocates of it. Although it sounds like common sense, the theory was practically ignored when first introduced. Fortunately, now it is widely accepted by law enforcement professionals and government leaders across the country. Very much a part of most community policing programs, "broken windows" is credited by many criminologists with partial responsibility for the decline in the overall national crime rate. A basic tenet of the philosophy is that everyone in the neighborhood bears responsibility for maintaining the health and safety of the neighborhood.

The question "Who paints a rented house?" is one we have employed to provoke awareness in crime prevention programs. The concepts of shared community responsibility and looking out for your neighbors are not new. They can be traced back thousands of years through many cultures. But somewhere along the way, we lost some of our commitment to each other.

We suggest that you adopt the "broken windows" approach as one of the foundation rules for safety practice in your community. It's more than a metaphor.

45. ADOPTING THE
"BROKEN WINDOWS" APPROACH

If you want to keep "big" crimes from taking place in your community, work to prevent the "little" crimes.

Our families share the house rule "Clean as you go." We believe it prevents all of our kids from letting small messes grow into bigger messes. The same is true with criminal activity. Crime occurs less often in places that are neat, orderly, well lit, and well kept. Most criminals are opportunists—don't let them take advantage of a situation you could have mitigated. The "broken windows" metaphor is a powerful illustration. Allowing decay and dilapidation is an invitation for minor crimes that can grow into major offenses.

Take the time to drive through a run-down neighborhood with your children. Point out graffiti, abandoned cars, open piles of trash, broken windows. Explain that all those "small" problems create an atmosphere conducive to larger ones.

▸ Police your own yard and street. If a strange car appears and remains abandoned, call the police or zoning office. If graffiti appears, do the same. If trash is strewn about, notify the city or county manager's office.

Keep an eye on any unattended or poorly maintained property. Too often, criminals will claim such an area to conduct their activities. If there is one close to your home, report it to local government officials. If nothing is done, follow up. If no action is taken, call a reporter from the local television station or newspaper and voice your concerns.

46. EXPRESSING CONCERNS

Make it a habit to express concerns about safety problems.

We recently heard a police officer give a talk about the importance of being tuned into the community. He had been assigned to a local high school and overheard several teachers discussing "The Dungeon." It turned out that the school was built on top of a maze of tunnels, about which he knew nothing. Staff, students, and people who grew up in the area, on the other hand, all knew about the tunnels. Police know an awful lot about your community, but often you and your neighbors know more about specific areas and their idiosyncrasies. Communication is vital to community safety. Give the professionals the information they need to protect you.

► If you have a neighborhood association that holds regular meetings, invite a representative from the police department or sheriff's office to come to a meeting at least once a year. Share your concerns with her and ask her to share crime analysis information she has about your area.

☎ Establish a phone tree for your neighborhood to be used in the event of an emergency. As soon as it's established, try it out to make sure it works. Then update it at least annually.

► Request that the police department or sheriff's office call a designated person in your neighborhood should any significant crime risk arise.

47. INVOLVING PUBLIC OFFICIALS

Teach your children that police and other public officials are here to assist us.

Children recognize power when they see it. They, like many of us, tend to think of public officials as powerful people whom they should not approach. In fact, you need to teach your children just the opposite— that all officials are in the business of public service and should be accessible to all members of the public, including children.

✓ Find out the names of your city or county manager; police chief or sheriff; members of the city council and school board; and state and federal legislators.

► Keep a list of their names and phone numbers in a prominent place (e.g., on the refrigerator or family corkboard).

☎ Call them to voice concerns if you have them, or to compliment them if things are going well. Believe us, they want to hear from you, and they or their staff will take note of your input.

► Teach your child, when she is calling a public official, that she needs to state her name, where she lives, and the purpose of her call.

► If you are calling to voice a concern, always ask that the official get back to you within a stated time period (e.g., two weeks) to let you know the outcome. Be reasonable, but be insistent. Persistence pays off.

48. SHOPPING SAFETY

Reduce your safety risk while shopping by assessing your surroundings.

It happens every holiday: a harried, distracted shopper exits a mall in the evening. As she juggles her many bags and boxes to search for her keys, a thief takes advantage of the opportunity and grabs her purse. Some people would say she's lucky he didn't harm her. We say no victim of crime is lucky, because no crime is acceptable. And while she didn't invite the crime, she failed to act in a way that could have prevented it.

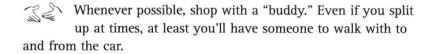 Whenever possible, shop with a "buddy." Even if you split up at times, at least you'll have someone to walk with to and from the car.

▸ Call your police chief or sheriff and ask if your mall or commercial neighborhood participates in a "mall watch" or "business watch" program, in which shopkeepers and owners of businesses routinely keep an eye open for suspicious activity and notify the police when necessary. If not, suggest that police talk to the owners or managers about doing so.

▸ Thieves love the hustle and bustle of crowds, where it's easier to jostle someone, steal a wallet or purse, and get lost immediately. Make sure in a crowded situation that your wallet or purse is secure. Wear the strap of your bag across your body hanging from one shoulder and turn the bag's opening in toward your body. Don't wear a wallet in your hip pocket. Carry it inside your jacket or in a front pocket.

Park in well-lighted, high-traffic areas. If that's not possible, don't walk to the car alone. Find a police or security officer and request assistance.

49. GROCERY STORE SAFETY

Do not leave personal belongings unattended in your shopping cart.

It's the end of a long day and you're tired. On the way home, you stop at the grocery store to pick up a couple of items. You rest your purse in the child seat of the shopping cart. The trouble is, someone else is in the store to pick up a couple of things, too, but she's not shopping for groceries. She is shopping for opportunities to create crime victims.

⊘ Don't ever put your purse in your shopping cart. Carry it over your shoulder or across your chest with the opening against your body.

► Don't think that laying your coat over your purse will protect it from thieves. They know far more tricks than you. You might lose both your coat and your purse.

► If you have purchased medication at the pharmacy, don't put it in the grocery cart. Immediately place it in your purse or pocket, or buy it at the end of your shopping excursion so you can take it out to the car right away.

► Don't carry your money or wallet in an open jacket pocket that's easily visible or accessible to others.

🔓 Don't leave your car unlocked when you are going into the store "only for a minute." That's all the time it takes a thief to steal your cell phone, CDs or tapes, or anything else he wants out of your vehicle—or the car itself.

► There are criminals who will take advantage of you as you walk, laden with groceries, to your car. If possible, have a store clerk accompany you. If not, keep your eyes open and have your keys ready.

50. PARKING DECKS AND GARAGES

Avoid multilevel parking decks or garages when possible. Park only in well-lighted, well-traveled, open areas.

Parking decks and garages are usually built for the convenience of businesses, not people. Most are not people-friendly. Only recently have architects begun incorporating Crime Prevention Through Environmental Design (CPTED) principles into the plans. Criminals know this. They like dark alleys and lonely parking garages, so when you must use one, think like a criminal. Then act to protect yourself.

► Study the garage as you enter it. Make sure you are comfortable with the level of lighting. If not, find another place to park.

► Park as close as possible to an exit.

► Park on the floor as close to ground level as you can get.

► Don't use the stairwell unless it is visible to people on the street or in nearby buildings.

👁 Look around cars as you walk to yours.

► Don't walk to your car alone if you have any concerns about your safety.

► Have your keys in your hand when you enter the garage.

⚒ Carry a loud whistle on your key chain. Use it when threatened.

51. HOUSES OF WORSHIP

Don't let yourself become a victim of crime just because you think crime doesn't occur in houses of worship.

Several years ago, there was a predator in a nearby city who knew how to find women alone. He looked for church employees who often worked alone well into the evening in large, unlocked, and otherwise unoccupied buildings. They were easy targets. You may feel safe in your church, but so do criminals.

If you are alone in the building, keep all the doors locked if possible. If not, unlock only the one in your line of sight or range of hearing.

► Churches are notorious for passing out keys to nearly everyone. It's great for convenience, but not for security. Ask your pastor or head layperson to identify all key holders and manage the limited dissemination of new keys.

If you sing in a choir, don't leave your handbag in open view in the practice room while you are in the sanctuary for a service or mass. Unfortunately, that's an open invitation for a thief.

► Ask your pastor or head layperson to prominently post the schedule of all church and community meetings regularly held in your building so that members will know who should be there and why. Your house of worship is probably open to persons other than members of your congregation.

5 2 .   P U B L I C   B U I L D I N G S

Don't let your guard down in public buildings.

Several years ago, a university hospital near us experienced a rash of crime. Jewelry was stolen from patients, drugs disappeared from cabinets, visitors' possessions vanished. A police officer with the university conducted a safety assessment, and by tightening up procedures and instituting a public-awareness campaign, the hospital cut crime significantly.

▸ People come and go in public buildings, often with little oversight. Remember that when you are in one of those buildings, you are sharing it with dozens or even hundreds of strangers. One of them could be a criminal looking for opportunity.

▸ If you are a patient in a hospital, leave your jewelry and cash at home. If you receive a valuable gift, have someone take it home for you the day you get it.

🚫 If you are visiting a patient in the hospital, do not leave your purse or other valuables unattended, even for a minute.

▸ If you are using the public or university library, do not leave your purse or other valuables on a study carrel or table.

👪 Teach your children to make a mental note of emergency exits and stairways, the number of floors in the building, and the general layout of the floor they're on.

53. BANKING AND ATMS

When you visit your automated teller machine (ATM), make sure you're the one who gets your cash.

Several years ago, a rash of robberies occurred at ATMs in our area. One inventive criminal simply waited until dark, crawled onto the roof overhanging the ATM machine, and waited for the right customer to come along, usually a lone female. He'd jump her, take the cash (and any jewelry he wanted), then melt into the darkness. Lucky for the rest of us, the banking industry has undertaken several measures designed to increase security at these locations (more CPTED). Still, if you must use an ATM in an isolated location or late at night, you may be playing with fire.

- ► Remember, most banks originally located ATMs based on marketing strategies, not on customer safety.

 Whenever possible, use an ATM in a well-lighted, high-traffic area.

- Avoid ATMs that are not visible from the street, have overgrown shrubbery, or are not well lighted.

- If you must use an ATM after dark, use only the drive-through kind.

  👁 Drive around the perimeter first and look for anything or anyone unusual.

- Keep your car doors locked and open your window only enough to complete your transaction.

- Conduct only absolutely necessary transactions after dark or in isolated locations.

- Once you have completed your transaction, pull away from the ATM. Don't sit there and count your money with your window still open.

54. PARKS AND
RECREATIONAL AREAS

Avoid parks at times when they can be isolated havens for criminal activity.

Most parks close down at sunset for good reason. The safety risk increases dramatically after dark. Patrols and organized activities reduce such risk. Educational and recreation programs, coordinated by paid staff or volunteers in well-lit areas, enable parks to be used for longer hours while increasing the safety of users.

► Call your police chief or sheriff and ask about crime patterns and rates in and around the parks you and your family frequent.

► Ask park staff whether the neighborhood surrounding the park has established a "park watch" program. These programs train volunteers to look for and report any suspicious activity.

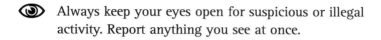 Always keep your eyes open for suspicious or illegal activity. Report anything you see at once.

► If you are a regular user of any particular part of the park—the jogging trail or a basketball court, for example—look for ways the area can be improved for safety. Does underbrush need to be cleared? Is there broken glass that should be cleaned up?

► Be a good neighbor: perform small maintenance chores—such as picking up litter—yourself or with a few friends, or volunteer with the parks department to organize a work day for larger projects.

 Whenever possible, use the park facility with a buddy or two, especially if you are using it after dark.

► Avoid routine. Don't always walk the same path or route at the same time day after day.

55. PREVENTING ABDUCTION

Never, ever let a stranger force you into a car or a building. Scream, flail, try to run, but do not get in unless you are certain resisting will result in serious bodily harm.

This is a much too frequent news story: recently, the media carried an account of a teenage girl who was found murdered two weeks after she disappeared while out walking her dog. There can be no more frightening nightmare for a parent. Teach your kids now, and remind them on a regular basis, what to do if approached by a stranger. It's good, of course, to have faith in people, and most people are trustworthy, but when it comes to your kids, it's far better to be safe than sorry. The damage inflicted by a child predator can last a lifetime.

▸ Strangers are found in small towns as well as large cities. No matter how comfortable your child feels, he needs to know that strangers are strangers and should be treated with firm politeness and healthy skepticism.

▸ Teach your child never, ever to go willingly into a vehicle or building with a stranger. If he is being forced, it's far better for him to scream, fight, or do whatever he can to attract attention to the situation.

Identify for your child other adults who might pick him up for you in any given situation, such as sporting events or in an emergency. Make sure they are people both you and your child trust. Give each person a note, business card, or other token with some unique marking or characteristic. Train your child to ask for it as your code for safety.

- Criminals who prey on children are well versed in what works. Tell your youngster not to believe any stranger or even acquaintance who says he is picking your child up for you.

Always impress upon your children that they can tell you anything about any adult, even if it's something about which a favorite uncle or babysitter has sworn them to secrecy.

56. PROTECTING YOUR IDENTITY

Protect your identity and the personal identifying information you carry.

In many ways, life is so much more convenient than it was even twenty years ago. We carry credit cards, debit cards, phone cards, and automatic teller cards. Electronics facilitate (some say control) our lives. Video phones are becoming more common, and there are more television channels available than we can possibly watch. Pagers, cell phones, and a host of other electronic communication aids allow us to reach virtually anyone, anywhere, anytime. We have video cameras, personal computers, laptops, electronic notebooks, Personal Digital Assistants (PDAs), and the Internet. We can access money, goods and services, and each other almost instantly. Unfortunately, so can criminals.

With increased convenience and access comes increased risk. Details about your personal life are available to almost anyone at the touch of a button or the stroke of a key. If you carry too much personal information with you, and your purse or wallet is stolen, your entire identity may be stolen as well. Criminals are increasingly taking advantage of information accessibility. Don't become one of their victims.

⊘ Guard your social security number. Do not carry it with you. Do not have it printed on your checks. Do not give it to clerks.

▸ Some states use the social security number as the driver's license number. If you live in one of those states, check to see if you can have an alternative number assigned to you.

- Do not carry PINs (personal identification numbers) with you. Memorize them and make them difficult enough that a stranger can't figure them out. For example, do not use your birth date or part of your address or phone number as your PIN.

When you are not carrying them, make sure your wallet, briefcase, purse, and any other item that contains identifying information about you and your finances are kept in a secure place.

- Be certain that credit card receipts find their way into your bag or hand and that carbon papers, if used, are destroyed.

- Limit access to your credit card numbers to vendors and locations you feel certain are secure.

- Guard your identification as carefully as you protect your person.

57. SENIOR CITIZEN SAFETY

Be mindful and promote the awareness that senior citizens are particularly vulnerable to safety threats.

A few winters ago, an unexpected and unusual ice storm hit our region just two days before Christmas. Large parts of the state were without power for days. Compounding the problem, downed trees made many roads impassable. Weather conditions such as ice, snow, floods, or high winds can impact elderly people especially hard—particularly those who live in rural areas or away from family members. The same is true for crime. Senior citizens are often targeted by con artists and others who make an illegal living at the expense of others.

▸ Make sure there is someone close by your elderly relatives who will check on them in the event of bad weather, criminal activity, or other emergencies.

✓ Check with your local power company to see whether it offers any kind of senior-citizen alert program when power outages occur.

☎ Call your police department or sheriff's office and determine what kinds of programs are offered to senior citizens.

▸ Student and youth community organizations are often looking for service projects. If you or your child is part of a scout troop or a similar organization, suggest that it take on a senior-citizen alert program as its long-term project.

▸ Find out if your local hospital offers alert programs for the elderly.

58. CONTROLLING ACCESS

Enhance the safety of your community through environmental design.

When do you feel safer? Walking alone down a street shrouded in darkness or strolling down a well-lit thoroughfare? Criminals prefer the cover of darkness; most of the rest of us don't. They like dark alleys and alcoves where they can be concealed. We don't. They like overgrown shrubs where they can escape detection. We like open areas with no surprises. They like areas that are nondescript; we prefer to know where we are at all times. Keep this in mind where and when you move around your community. Think Crime Prevention Through Environmental Design (CPTED).

Make it a habit everywhere you go in your community to look at the lighting. If it is inadequate in public places, call your police chief or sheriff and tell him so. Use the CPTED buzzword.

- Study the commercial areas you and your family frequent. Check to see if address numbers are prominently displayed. If not, mention your concern to the business or to the police.

- As you travel in your community at night, look at the operating hours of various businesses. If any seem to be generating crime or disorder, partly because of their hours of operation, call the Chamber of Commerce, the Retail Merchants Association, or local government leaders to discuss your concerns.

Keep your eyes open to potential traffic-control problems. If cruising is a problem, call your chief to ask that patrols be stepped up or other measures taken.

59. DEALING WITH CRUISING

Find out what you can do to reduce cruising in your community.

Cruising—a centerpiece of the 1972 movie classic *American Graffiti*—gave teenagers a way to see and be seen. It was fun. Chances are you did it. We did.

As long as kids have had cars they've cruised, and today's teens are no different. They cruise to see and be seen, but when their activities lead to other problems like traffic congestion, fights, or public intoxication, then it becomes a safety threat.

It's easy to find the spot kids have chosen to cruise; it's more difficult to change it.

▶ If your town or city is experiencing a cruising problem, the first thing to do is find out why the kids are cruising. Your school or police department can survey teens to learn why they cruise and why they've picked that particular spot.

Ask your police department to conduct lighting and traffic surveys of the area to make sure that lighting is adequate and that appropriate traffic signals are in place.

Ask police to set up additional patrols of the area during the hours kids cruise.

► Some localities or cruise spots have chosen to play classical music very loudly to discourage kids from congregating.

► Involve kids in the solution. Find out what they recommend be done about the situation.

► If kids are cruising because they have nothing else to do, check with the local chamber of commerce, YMCA, or recreation department to determine whether additional organized activities can be offered.

60. REVITALIZING HOT SPOTS

Take back your neighborhood.

Typically, fewer than 5 percent of the addresses in a city are responsible for half the crime that occurs. You may not live in a neighborhood plagued by drug trafficking, burglaries, and other crimes, but chances are they exist not too far away. Any neighborhood that faces these problems is not only breeding fear and frustration; it is also bleeding resources from other, more positive activities. Find out what challenges law enforcement officials are facing and what you can do to help. Officers can't do it alone, and we shouldn't expect them to.

☎ High-crime locations are often referred to as "hot spots." Call your police department to see if it keeps track of such areas and where they are.

► If any of these locations are businesses, ask if they are in violation of any fire, health, or safety codes or regulations. If so, ask what steps can be taken to bring them into compliance.

► Ask if community organizations can assist law enforcement in cleaning up a hot spot—painting over graffiti or cleaning up a park as a community service project.

✓ Check with your local chamber of commerce to see if it has any programs to address hot spots in your city or county.

► Ask your local newspaper or television station to run a series on local hot spots to bring attention to the problem.

61. PARENTAL ACCOUNTABILITY

Work to make sure parents in your locality are held accountable for the actions of their children.

Anyone who makes a choice to become a parent incurs a whole new level of responsibility and accountability. Children have to be taught that their behavior can help or hurt them and others. Parents can make a choice. By your example and supervision, you can make safety a priority in your child's life. You can teach him to make responsible decisions, or you can risk being held accountable when he doesn't.

✓ Call your local prosecutor's office and find out whether a state law or local ordinance holds parents accountable for the actions of their dependent children. If so, ask what the sanctions are and whether they are enforced. If not, consider writing the appropriate council members or legislators to lobby for such a law.

► Also ask whether there are any state laws on the books that force parents to pay restitution for damage inflicted by their children.

☎ Call your local school district and ask about policies holding parents accountable for their children's behavior in school. Again, find out what the sanctions are for the parents and the kids.

► Publicize the information you receive through your PTA/PTO or community organization. Seek help from local media to get the word out.

62. WORKING WITH YOUR LOCAL MEDIA

Engage your local media to highlight concerns and successes.

A retired detective we know used to say, "In order to get to the pearl, you have to irritate the oyster." Sometimes the best way to change a situation is to manipulate it a little. Ours has become a media-saturated society. You can use this fact to your advantage, because television, radio, and print media are always looking for good stories. And in this competitive environment, many of them have grown much more "public friendly." One of the best community-safety tools you have is the media. Nothing gets the word out faster.

☎ Call your local newspaper and ask for the public-affairs editor or the community reporter. Suggest specific story ideas such as juvenile restitution or parental accountability.

▸ Do the same with your local television station.

▸ Learn the local media's policies on public service announcements (PSAs).

☎ Call your police department and talk with the crime prevention officer or school resource officer. See if he has any ideas about stories to highlight safety problems or successes.

▸ Kids often have very definite safety concerns. Check with the journalism teacher at the local high school to see if she is interested in working with the media on school or community safety issues.

▸ If you are not satisfied with answers you get from local officials, let the media know. They may want to pursue the issue, especially if you convince them it involves a valid safety concern.

at work

Millions of us spend thousands of hours a year away from family and friends while we are at work. Being on the job, taking care of business, providing for our loved ones—some of us love it; many of us work only because we have to. If we must work, need we also be concerned about our safety on the job?

Yes and no. Concerned, but not overly concerned. Aware, but not preoccupied.

Unless you are a firefighter or police officer, an acrobat or race-car driver, a steel worker or jailer, you probably have not accepted danger as a part of your work routine. The excitement of the near-death experience may be something you crave with your weekend hobby, but not at work. In fact, just getting to work may present safety concerns. Commuting on the highways and walking from the parking deck involve routines that can be threatening if we don't give some thought to safety.

We don't have to wear hard hats or be subject to stringent OSHA regulations to grow more safety conscious. From construction site to high-rise to daycare center, safety challenges exist in our workplaces about which we should be aware. And safety practices should be something we observe for our own benefit as well as for the benefit of those around us—colleagues, fellow commuters, clients, and customers.

We can all be safer at work if we all work at being safe.

63. SAFE ROUTES TO WORK

Study the exterior of the building you work in to assess potential threats to your safety.

Most of us choose our employer, but we can't always choose the location or building in which we work. What we can do is select the safest routes to and from work and reduce our risk of becoming victims of workplace crime.

 If you walk to work, use only well-lighted streets or walkways. If possible, walk with a buddy.

▸ If you drive to work, park as close to your building as possible.

▸ Avoid poorly lit parking areas or areas hidden from view by landscaping, hills, or fences.

Know who else is around. Look for familiar cars and faces. Try to time your arrival and departure to coincide with the schedules of others.

▸ If you leave work late and don't feel comfortable walking to your car by yourself, request an escort. Any employer who denies such a request is doing so at his own legal peril.

If sidewalks and pathways are well lighted, use them. Don't opt for shortcuts through wooded, overgrown, or abandoned areas.

64 . AVOIDING DARKNESS

Whenever possible,
avoid darkness at work.

Most of us feel more comfortable in light and at least a little appre-hensive in the dark. This is especially true when we aren't completely sure of our surroundings. Criminals often play on our fears and enhance their own chances of success by doing their work under the cover of darkness. Whenever you have the choice, pick light over dark. And as often as you can, ensure that you have a choice.

► If you work into the night, avoid long dark hallways and stairwells.

If you're working alone or away from others, turn on as many lights as you can in your workspace and the spaces around you.

► If you work late on a fairly regular basis, make sure yours isn't the only light on in a building or an area. If an intruder is watching, it could increase your chances of becoming a victim.

► Vary your routine. Many of us are such creatures of habit that a criminal could set his watch by our movements. Don't be that regular.

If you have to move at night from one part of a building to another, call for an escort first. If that's not possible, turn on lights as you go.

► Act purposeful, confident, and in control. Doing so not only enhances your state of mind, studies show it may deter a crimi-nal. Given the choice, most criminals will choose a timid, fright-ened victim over an intent, self-assured individual.

65. RESTROOM SAFETY

Stay safety conscious in restrooms.

Several years ago, on the campus of a community college, a peeping tom took advantage of an isolated building during evening classes. He hid in a stall in the women's restroom, waiting for someone to use the stall next to it, then watched her over the partition. Most of his victims never even knew he was there or realized the potential danger of the situation.

► Always be aware of your surroundings in or near a restroom.

► If you must use a workplace or public restroom, look for one that is in a high-traffic area.

 If you can lock the outside door, do so.

► Always scan the area and leave at once if anything makes you uncomfortable.

⊘ Do not hang your purse, coat, or other valuables on a door hook unless the hook is in the middle of the door, out of reach of anyone walking by.

⊘ Do not remove your jewelry while standing at the sink in a public restroom.

66. AVERTING
STRANGER DANGER

Make it a habit to maintain a respectful distance between you and strangers.

If your work situation calls for constant interaction with strangers, or if you work for a big company, you may spend a large part of your workday with people you don't really know. While most people are honest and trustworthy, you can't trust everyone. And you should not. It is foolhardy to put yourself at undue risk.

▸ Do not divulge your personal habits, living arrangements, or travel plans to fellow workers unless you know them very well.

▸ Try to avoid working late into the night with another employee unless you know the person or someone you trust can vouch for him.

▸ Don't reveal information about your personal finances in the office where others can overhear you. For example, don't give out credit card numbers over the phone when others are nearby.

If for some reason you feel uneasy around a coworker, remain cautious—at least until his actions and conduct have allayed your fears.

67. WORKPLACE TEAMS

Work together to keep your workplace safe.

Have you ever had to leave work in a rush because of a sick child or some other emergency? Did you have time to put everything away or did you wonder later what you had left out or open? In the event of an emergency or a need to leave work quickly, most of us tend to go on autopilot, automatically closing files, shutting off equipment, doing whatever is necessary to close up shop. But sometimes we forget. That's when the cooperation that comes from having a "buddy" really pays off.

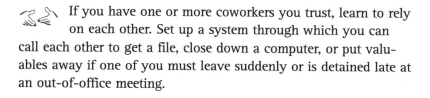 If you have one or more coworkers you trust, learn to rely on each other. Set up a system through which you can call each other to get a file, close down a computer, or put valuables away if one of you must leave suddenly or is detained late at an out-of-office meeting.

- Consider setting up a system by which you can check on each other in case one of you is late for work or something unforeseen happens.

- Establish a routine where you check on each other before leaving so you'll know if someone is working late and vice versa.

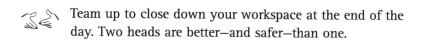 Team up to close down your workspace at the end of the day. Two heads are better—and safer—than one.

68. SECURING YOUR OFFICE

Keep your office or workspace as secure as possible.

Several years ago, Donna occupied a workspace that became the favorite "break spot" for the nighttime cleaning crew, apparently because it offered a direct line of vision to the elevators. She could not keep the space wholly secure, so instead, chose to keep nothing of value in her work area.

► If you have to or choose to keep valuables at work, request a desk, file cabinet, or some kind of case that locks.

► Make it a habit to lock up your belongings when you leave each evening.

When you leave your desk or work area for a few minutes, don't assume that your belongings will be secure. Put them under lock and key or take them with you. At the very least, have your "buddy" keep an eye on your things.

► Don't assume that your work products are secure, either. If you are working on an assignment that is confidential, lock it up or take it with you.

If you have voice mail, make sure that no one can discover your voice-mail access code simply by hitting the redial button.

69. ESTABLISHING
WORKSPACE BOUNDARIES

Maintain your personal workspace so that everyone knows it is yours.

A no-nonsense police captain we knew years ago painted his office an unusual and unpleasant shade of green. No one liked it, which is why he said he did it. He didn't want anyone lingering in his office too long. But the paint job had an added effect. Everyone knew that office belonged to him, and no one else felt comfortable being in there when he wasn't. Specialists in CPTED tell us that setting up boundaries will define areas of personal and public space. Use that to your advantage by delineating your personal workspace as much as possible. People will be less likely to cross it.

Define your work area. Use a different color carpet or flooring, if possible, or create a boundary with plants or file cabinets.

▸ Make your space distinctive. You may not be able to paint it any color you choose, but you can hang pictures or set out personal items.

▸ Set some of your belongings along the perimeter of your space so that the boundaries are clear.

▸ Locate your phone where you have the greatest privacy possible while you are talking.

▸ If you have an office with a door, don't be afraid to close it occasionally to help establish your space.

70. ALTERING
WORKPLACE ROUTINES

Change your work habits
and routines once in a while.

Do you leave the house for work at about the same time every day? Do you try to park in the same spot or catch the same bus? Do you sit in the same seat on the commuter train?

We live by habit. It keeps our lives from becoming too chaotic. Unfortunately, it also increases the opportunity for us to become victims of crime. Think a moment about the many things you do daily the same way, at the same time. Now think about how easy it would be for a stalker to follow you, charting your habits and routines.

▸ Try to change your work routines periodically. It will keep you from becoming too complacent to potential safety risks, and it will hinder a criminal's attempt to learn your schedule.

✓ Exchange perspectives every now and then. Mentally, walk a mile in a stalker's shoes. Would you make an easy target? Change any custom you follow that makes you vulnerable.

71 . WORKING ALONE

If you must work alone at night, take extra precautions for your personal safety.

Several years ago, a young woman in a small rural city was working alone in a convenience store. The town was friendly, the crime rates low—it was considered a very safe place. But that night, as she was working, a stranger appeared in the store. She became uncomfortable enough to call the police as soon as he left. By the time a patrol car arrived moments later, she had disappeared. She was never found and never heard from again.

► If you work alone in a gas station, convenience store, or any retail establishment in an isolated area, make sure your supervisor has a safety plan.

Be certain all entrances except the main one, in your line of vision, are locked.

► Keep the door keys handy and practice locking up quickly.

Have a friend or family member call to check on you periodically, or have a regular call-in time when you contact them.

► Be certain emergency numbers are posted near the telephone.

► If there isn't a second telephone in a back room to which you may retreat if threatened, ask that one be installed, or consider carrying a cell phone with you at all times.

72. HEEDING
EARLY WARNING SIGNS

Watch for warning signs or changes in the behavior of your coworkers.

You can't be responsible for everyone's behavior at work, and you shouldn't be. But events that take place there profoundly affect our lives. Whether you work in a large corporation, a small business, or a midsize establishment, it pays to be mindful of your coworkers. You aren't being nosy; you are practicing workplace safety.

Watch for significant changes in behavior such as social withdrawal, sudden irrational anger, feelings of persecution, depression, lack of attentiveness, or significant failure in performance.

- If you see a risky pattern emerging, talk to the individual. If it persists and begins to impact others, talk to your supervisor or your coworker's supervisor confidentially.

- If you are in a supervisory position and someone brings such a matter to your attention, it is your responsibility to act on those concerns.

If you work in a business or industry that is inherently dangerous, such as on a construction site where heavy machinery is being operated, it is especially important to do everything you can to reduce the risk for harm.

73. PREPARING FOR EMERGENCIES

Prepare for emergencies in the workplace just as you once did in school.

Remember the fire drills we had in school? Maybe you even took part in weather-related practice drills. We adults need to do the same. You probably spend as much time at work as you do anyplace else, so the safety of that environment should be as important to you as the safety of your home. Don't abdicate the responsibility to others, or assume that someone else will take charge in the event of an emergency. You need to know what to do. Proper training and practice are the keys to ensuring you will.

✓ Most commercial buildings are required to post escape routes. Take the time to know where they are displayed and how they pertain to you.

▸ Pay special attention to the parts of the building you frequent most.

👁 Note the location(s) of the fire alarms and fire extinguishers.

▸ Find out how to contact building security. In the event of an emergency, you may be the first one to make a call.

▸ Establish an emergency coordinator in your business, building, or organization and some means of emergency communication.

► Make sure you know where first aid equipment is located at work, or keep some basic supplies handy in your workstation or office.

Maintain a buddy system, either formally or informally. It is important to know who is in the building at any given time. Watch out for each other.

► Keep a radio (battery operated) at work so you can follow official reports should you lose electricity.

► First, assist anyone who is disabled and might have trouble responding properly to an emergency.

► Establish a central point away from the building where you can all meet should an emergency evacuation occur. Use the buddy system to make sure everyone is accounted for.

at play

If work is part of being a "responsible adult," play is a critical aspect of life for "children" from age nine months to ninety years. We need to relax, unwind, work out, push the limits, get away from it all. Unless our playtime activity is inherently dangerous, thoughts of safety are not close at hand when we seek the exercise, relaxation, and other benefits—physical, mental, emotional—of play. But it is precisely during the times when we aren't thinking "safety first" that accidents happen or criminals take advantage of opportunity.

Whether we are engaged in a strenuous sport or a walk in the woods, safety consciousness is not only appropriate, it is essential. Every year thousands are hurt in leisure-time accidents that could have been prevented. Hundreds become victims of crime when they let their guard down during activities that are meant to provide an escape from the complexities and anxieties of the "real world." But think about it for a moment: when we have assumed the risk for an activity we have undertaken voluntarily—for fun, for fitness, for family unity—isn't it our responsibility to provide as safe an experience as possible?

Granted, concentrating on safety measures is a given when we are mountain climbing or skydiving, but must safety really be a concern during evening strolls through the neighborhood and while on family camping trips?

Absolutely. You could bet your life on it. But don't. Be smart. Play safe.

74. FIRST AID

Make first aid a primary consideration for any leisure activity.

As much as we can plan events and activities and seek to ensure the safety of everyone involved, even the best plans sometimes go awry. That's when first aid may be required. Whether you are boating or braving the cold, swimming or skiing, fishing or floating in a pool, first aid should always be at the ready.

✓ Keep a first aid kit in your home at all times. Check it regularly and conduct a full inventory at least twice a year (on the same days you change your clocks and replace your smoke-detector batteries) to replace or add materials.

► Put together a portable first aid kit that you can carry with you whenever you go on a trip—whether daylong or overnight.

Talk with your children about the items to be included in a basic first aid kit and how to use them so they know how to respond to accidents.

► Add items to your first aid kit as needed for specific trips or activities. For example, if you are going to be outside all day, you may wish to add sunscreen and a burn lotion.

► As a family, decide when and where you need first aid kits.

75. KEEPING IN TOUCH

Always plan a means of communication.

We are living in the information age and the age of instant communication. While that can sometimes make us crazy, it serves us well most of the time and provides us incredible freedom. As you go about your leisure activities, consider the importance of communication. There are many ways to stay in touch, high-tech and otherwise.

Consider establishing a family signal. In Bruce's family, it's a distinctive whistle. The kids know that when they hear it, the parents want them to come immediately. When the adults hear it, they must respond as well.

- Pagers are relatively inexpensive and can be used by children as well as adults. Whether a basic model or state-of-the-art, they allow us to almost instantly contact one another in the event of an emergency.

- Cell phones were nearly unheard of just a decade ago. Today they are accessible to millions of Americans. They provide one of the best means of instant communication.

Walkie-talkies don't have the range of cell phones, but nor do they carry the high price tag. If your family is active, walkie-talkies may be the ideal way to stay in touch—during games, at the beach, hiking, or just bumming around.

- Citizen band radios (CBs) are not as popular as they once were, but they provide a fairly inexpensive way to communicate at reasonably close range, especially car-to-car on the highway.

76. WEATHER-PROOFING
YOUR RECREATION PLANS

Pay special attention to weather safety precautions to keep nature from ruining your fun.

We each grew up in cold weather and loved it. Tobogganing, skating, and skiing were essential parts of our winter play. It was never too cold or too snowy to have fun. Sun worshippers feel the same about summer's heat. Sports and other leisure activities can be enjoyed any time of year in all but the most severe weather—with proper precautions and attention. Otherwise, the results can be harmful, even fatal.

Always listen to weather and condition reports and prepare accordingly. Weather specialists' predictions may not always be right, but they are basing their reports on sophisticated scientific factors unknown to most of us. Don't ignore weather warnings.

▸ Consider investing in a battery-operated weather radio. They're relatively inexpensive and offer more detail than most network broadcasts.

▸ Dress in layers. It's easier to maintain an optimum temperature and comfort level if you can adapt to changing conditions.

Because cold weather activities are inherently more dangerous than activities conducted in moderate weather, they're always safer when enjoyed with a buddy.

▸ Err on the side of caution. Don't under-dress, overexert yourself, or venture forth ill-prepared.

Don't allow yourself to become overheated or chilled. Our bodies will usually tell us when we're in trouble. Heed the warnings. Know when body temperature changes have become dangerous and act accordingly. Get out of the elements when you need a break, and never be too tough to seek medical assistance for yourself or others.

▸ Make sure each family member carries identification and some means of communication at all times.

77. ORGANIZING FOR SAFETY

When you organize children's activities, plan them around a framework of safety.

A special talent is required for organizing children's activities, and some parents and teachers appear to do it effortlessly. We've always secretly admired those individuals, partly because they inherently seem to cover all the bases—fun, learning, sportsmanship, and safety. Especially for parental peace of mind, safety should be a primary consideration in any organized group activity.

The most important safety factor is the buddy system. Make sure every child has a buddy for any organized activity, preferably a buddy she likes and trusts.

- Account for as many activities and as much time as you can. The more organized the activity, the less likely that something will go wrong.

- Establish a Plan B should your first plan go awry in some way.

- Make sure all the parents involved are fully aware of the planned activities.

Use a sufficient number of adults to keep the children under adult surveillance at all times. Specific assignments of children to adults should be made.

- Ensure that everyone knows what to do and whom to call in case of an emergency.

78. CHECKING
PLAYGROUND CONDITIONS

Examine and monitor your children's play areas for risks of crime or accident.

Children at play—like adults—become engrossed in whatever they are doing and tend to lose touch with what is going on around them. That's why it is our responsibility as parents to keep their play area as safe and secure as possible.

Bruce remembers thinking his mother had eyes in the back of her head. She seemed to be aware of her children's every move, all the time. The reality is we need more than eyes to keep youngsters safe today. We also need action. If you use public play spaces and equipment, it is up to you to ensure safe conditions and report any safety problems.

✓ If your child plays regularly in a park or playground, do what you can to keep it safe. Periodically check the area for broken glass, sharp metal, or other dangerous conditions.

► Make it a habit to check the equipment regularly. Are swing sets secure? Is the sandbox free from debris and trash? Has sand or some other material been placed below slides, swing sets, and jungle gyms?

► Pay particular attention to litter. Don't let it accumulate or over-flow from trash cans.

☀ If the park or recreation area is open and used at night, check the lighting. If any bulbs are broken or burned out, report the situation at once.

► Look at the landscaping. If there is any vegetation that obstructs your view or presents a threat to safety, report this also.

👁 Examine the perimeter of the play area. Is it secure? Are the boundaries well defined to deter trespassing? If possible, utilize play areas where access is controlled.

► Look closely at the surrounding area. Is there overgrown brush? Are there abandoned buildings nearby? Is the area bordered by a heavily traveled road? Keep your youngster as far from such risks as possible.

► Are possibly inappropriate users of the area present? If the playground is designed for young children, but teen or adult loiterers whose presence gives you an uneasy feeling are constantly about, report the condition, then remain aware to see if anything has been done about it.

Avoid running or walking in unfamiliar or dangerous surroundings.

We all know the rules for safe running or walking, but those of us who are die-hard exercise enthusiasts sometimes put safety considerations aside in order to maintain a workout schedule. While the short-term gains may be worthwhile, the results may not justify the risks we assume.

► Know your route. Know the traffic patterns, the location(s) of telephones, and the natural surveillance afforded by the route.

✓ If you are traveling, check with the hotel staff or your host to find the safest route to run or walk.

► Always let someone—
a family member,
colleague, or friend—
know your general time
frame and route. Again,
if you are traveling,
let the concierge or
desk clerk know you
are leaving for a run
or a walk.

- Always carry some form of identification such as a clothing label, business card, or driver's license. Even a hotel key will help identify you should an accident occur.

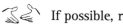 If possible, run or walk with a buddy.

- Whenever you can, run or walk during daylight or in well-lit areas.

- Consider carrying a walkie-talkie (if distance permits) or cell phone so someone is always within earshot, especially if you are in an unfamiliar area or out after dark.

- If you have any type of medical problem that could be exacerbated in the event of an injury or other emergency, consider carrying a medic alert card or wearing a bracelet.

- Make it a habit to wear some kind of reflective clothing.

- If you run or walk while listening to a portable walkman, consider the safety consequences. Is listening to your favorite tunes really more important than being able to hear a mugger sneaking up behind you or a truck running a red light?

80. CYCLING AND SKATING

Follow bicycling and skating safety tips.

Millions of children and adults enjoy the fun and freedom of cycling and skating sports. Unfortunately, thousands of these athletes are hurt each year in accidents that could have been prevented. On the other side of the coin, some terrible mishaps, fortunately, are averted with careful forethought. A man featured in his local news took up the practice of wearing a helmet when his children reached bicycling age. Although helmets were not required for adults, he wore one because he wanted to set an example for his kids. One day, he and his young son were casually riding a short distance on a paved, level bicycle path. Dad's front tire hit a small, barely visible rock. He flipped over the handlebars and landed on his head, crushing his helmet. He was so impressed with the damage to his helmet—which otherwise would likely have been enough damage to his head to result in some level of permanent disability—he contacted the local media. He wanted others to witness the real-life benefits of wearing a helmet, even on apparently "safe" rides.

Whether you are a novice or an X Games (extreme games) expert, following some simple rules for cycling and skating can keep you out of harm's way and ready for action.

Wear a helmet. Always. Every time. No serious cyclist or skater goes even the shortest distance without a helmet. Adults should follow their example and set one for their children. Helmets should be as much a habit as seat belts and child safety seats in vehicles.

► Make sure that your
and your kids' hel-
mets fit snugly and
properly, and impress
upon your kids the
importance of wear-
ing them according-
ly. A helmet worn
too loosely can result
in its coming off
during an accident;
one worn too far
back on the head
fails to protect the
forehead. An
employee at a rep-
utable recreational-
gear store can show
you how to adjust
the straps for a
perfect fit.

► Skateboarders and in-line skaters should wear protective wrist
guards and knee and elbow pads.

✔ A loose wheel can cause a serious accident. Ensure that
your family's bikes and skating gear are well maintained.
Many communities offer free bicycle-repair workshops for youth.

► Cyclists are usually subject to the same traffic regulations as automobiles. Find out the laws for cyclists in your town, and follow them.

► Use and teach your children to use hand signals.

Be predictable in your movements and defensive around vehicular traffic. Remain constantly alert and watchful for cars, other hazards, and pedestrians.

► Try always to ride or skate in designated bike lanes or on off-street bike paths.

If your community has no designated bike lanes or paths, call your local lawmakers and voice your concerns.

► Equip all family bikes with flashing reflectors on the back and bright headlights on the front. Check the batteries before each time you ride. Even if you don't plan to ride after dark, it's better to be safe in case you're caught out later than expected or in case the weather changes.

► Wear reflective clothing.

81. GYMS AND CLUBS

When you go to the gym or the club, leave your valuables at home.

Last year, a new gym opened in our community. Like many exercise facilities, this one caters to a wide range of individuals: college kids, middle-aged professionals, young mothers, twentysomething singles. Recently, in the middle of a weekday afternoon, several patrons returned to their cars to find the windows smashed and all their valuables missing. The thieves took advantage of an opportunity that is far too common. Many people don't carry valuables into the gym because they don't want them stolen. Instead, they lock them in their cars, assuming they'll be safe. Unfortunately, that's just the kind of thinking and conduct opportunistic criminals count on.

▶ When you go to the gym, leave your cash and your purse at home. Carry your driver's license separately.

▶ Don't leave CDs, cell phones, money, or jewelry in plain view in your vehicle.

Always lock your car doors and close your windows completely.

► Use a combination lock on your gym locker.

► Park as close to the building as possible.

 If possible, don't park beside any large vehicle that can block the view to your car. Try to park so that normal vehicular and pedestrian traffic have a clear view of your vehicle.

► Ask the gym staff if any problems have occurred in the building or in the parking lot.

If you feel unsafe walking to your car after your workout, request an escort or wait until other patrons are leaving.

82. WATER SPORTS

Don't take chances when it comes to water sports.

Thinking about taking a vacation? What location do you envision? There's something about water that appeals to almost everyone. Millions of us choose to spend our free time near oceans, rivers, lakes, and swimming pools. Such places are also where thousands of deaths occur each year, many of them preventable.

⊘ Don't swim alone or in unfamiliar water unless a lifeguard is present.

- Those who are not strong swimmers, especially children, should wear personal flotation devices (PFDs) when around water, particularly in surf where sudden changes in waves and rip currents can challenge even the most experienced swimmer.

- Don't dive unless you can see the bottom and a depth marker.

- If you are swimming at a club or neighborhood pool, know the rules and follow them. If no flotation toys are allowed in the water, for example, then don't use one. It could increase risk for you and others.

 If possible, swim and boat with a buddy.

- When in a boat or near the edge of deep or rushing water, always wear a life vest. Many accidents happen so quickly there is no time to put one on. And even the strongest swimmers are no match for white water or might be knocked unconscious in an accident.

If you frequent a beach, always watch out for broken glass or other debris.

- If you swim in a lake or river, be on the lookout for debris in the water, especially tree limbs or other dangerous objects that may be floating out of sight.

- Don't push yourself to the limit. Hundreds of swimmers drown each year from becoming exhausted.

Establish family rules
for theme parks.

Water parks, theme parks, and other specialty parks differ from other types of family activities, and they all require a family plan for safety. Most of them cover hundreds, perhaps thousands, of acres. It's easy to get lost or separated. Even though most large amusement parks are well managed for safety and employ staff trained to respond quickly in emergencies, it remains your responsibility to ensure that all family members know and practice the plan.

Most theme parks have extensive parking lots. Teach every member of your family to note the exact location of your parking spot. Often parking areas are marked with numbers or symbols. But that's not enough. Train your children to look for other nearby landmarks, too.

- Note the hours of park operation so that everyone is aware of closing time. Establish a meeting spot either near the center of the park, close by the gate, or at some familiar location.

▸ If your party splits up, you should arrange to meet at a specific location every couple of hours to check on one another.

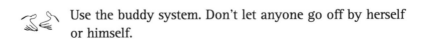 Show your children where they should go, or to whom, in the event of an emergency. Park personnel should be dressed in distinctive clothing. Information and first aid areas are clearly marked in most parks.

▸ Unless park rules prohibit them, consider carrying walkie-talkies to stay in contact with one another.

▸ Posted health considerations and minimum ages, heights, and weights are based on safety factors. Abide by them and teach your children to do the same.

▸ Most theme-park rides are quite safe, but that doesn't mean we can let our guard down. Talk to your children about what to do in the event of an accident or emergency, especially if you are in another part of the park.

▸ Don't let young children enter restrooms or wander through the park alone.

Use the buddy system. Don't let anyone go off by herself or himself.

▸ Make sure everyone in the group is carrying some form of identification.

84. CAMPING

Keep your campsite secure.

Camping is an all-American pastime and great fun. Campgrounds can be found in rural, suburban, and even urban areas. While they differ depending on their location and purpose, they share many characteristics and contain many of the same inherent safety risks. Attention to some basic rules can help avert accidents and unpleasantness.

► Familiarize yourself and your family or party with the rules of the park and the advisories pertaining to that area. Rangers and park personnel want you to have fun, but they know what you don't about their workplace. Pay attention to what they tell you.

► Whether you are camping in a tent, a conversion van, or a recreational vehicle, you are sharing space with dozens or hundreds of strangers—human and otherwise. Keep your campsite secure from intrusion and theft. It is your home away from home. Open food and valuables can attract unwanted visitors.

► Do not leave any valuables at the site if you depart the area and no adult is left behind.

⊘ Do not leave your children alone without an adult at the campsite. It's just as dangerous if no one is around as it is if surrounded by strangers.

☎ Consider carrying a cell phone with you. Remember to keep it charged.

⊘ Do not share your itinerary or travel plans with strangers just because they are camped in the site next to yours and appear friendly.

► Do not let children go to bathing or swimming areas or wander through the campground alone.

Plan to come home when you take a hike.

Whether you take a short walk through the woods, around the lake, down the beach, or spend days on mountain trails, there aren't many forms of outdoor exercise as satisfying as a hike. So much of what nature has to offer can be enjoyed while proceeding at our own pace on the path of our choice. But no matter where you are, planning and precaution are proper.

 Before you set out, let someone know where you are going and when you'll be back.

▸ Leave your name, route, and destination in park offices and trail registration boxes so that you can be located in the event of an emergency.

▸ Carry identification and some means of communication, a cell phone if you can.

✓ Be as familiar as possible with, or at least somewhat informed about, where you are going, where you will end up, and what you can expect to encounter along the way.

▸ Don't assume anything or be carelessly casual about whom or what you come upon. Not everyone may be there to enjoy nature.

▸ If you plan to be out for awhile, be prepared for sudden changes in weather. Storms and temperature drops can be exciting—but deadly.

- Be certain your footgear and attire are appropriate to protect you for the entire length of your hike.

- Carry water, food, and at least basic first aid items if you will
  be out more than two or three hours.

Reduce your risks in large crowds and close quarters by exercising simple safety precautions.

Spectator sports are as much a part of our culture as Mom and apple pie. On any given weekend, in any given city, thousands of Americans join other fans in rooting for their favorite sports figures. But there are others who frequent stadiums not to see the game but to take advantage of large crowds and the desire to enjoy oneself. When you relax at a stadium, don't let your guard down completely.

Place all valuables out of sight in your trunk and lock your car when you leave it. Better yet, leave no valuables in the car at all.

- Use a canvas or nylon bag with a zipper to carry your stadium blanket, field glasses, and anything else you might need. The zipper will prevent easy access to your belongings.

- Don't carry your purse or wallet where it can be easily taken from you in a large crowd.

- Don't leave valuable clothing or other items at your seat unattended.

Take note of police officers or security personnel so you know where they are should you need them quickly.

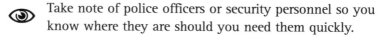

- ► Take note of escape routes and exits near your seat.

- ► Know the rules and regulations. Do not take alcoholic beverages into any stadium in which they are not allowed.

on the road

Millions of us love to travel, but when we do, safety challenges abound. How we confront them can make all the difference.

Perhaps we are no more vulnerable at any time than when traveling. Whether it is for work, fun, or school, in the air, on the land, or by sea, we are exposed to elements of danger—natural and manmade—when moving about that we otherwise never encounter. Part of the reason for this discomforting reality is that we lack our cocoon, our shell—the insulation that we call home. Another factor involves control.

When we are driving, in charge of our own machine while enjoying the freedom of the open road, we may feel we are masters of our fate, but in fact we don't escape threats to our safety. For we have no control over the hundreds of other vehicles we pass. So we learn to drive defensively and be on the lookout.

Often we travel with someone else operating the conveyance. Then our lives are quite literally in the hands of strangers. Does this mean we are totally at their mercy? Helpless? Or are there measures we can take, practices we may follow to reduce our exposure to harm?

Travel for most of us is a necessity. As we set forth on our journeys of minutes or miles, how do we reduce the hazards and minimize our vulnerability? Or can we?

The answer to these essential questions is of course we can.

We should be no more willing to accept tragedy resulting from crime, accidents, or weather on the road than we are at home, at work, or in our community. On the road as elsewhere, we can minimize our risks and reduce our chances of becoming a victim. Here, as in the other aspects of our lives, we must assume responsibility to make safety a priority.

87. AVOIDING
CAR BREAKDOWNS

Keep your car serviced to help keep you safe.

Remember your first car? You probably took great care of it. If back then you were more concerned with how you looked driving around in your car than with its safety, now you know better. You may not think of your car's service schedule as a safety feature, but one of the greatest threats to your safety is having your car break down on the side of the road. The risk of oncoming traffic, the threat of being a victim of crime, and the uncertainty of the environment are all factors that need to be considered as you travel. Most of these can be significantly minimized if your car is well maintained. Most states have annual or semiannual inspection laws. You may regard mandatory inspections as a nuisance, but that preventive maintenance also serves as insurance to protect you from other vehicles that might cause you harm.

▸ Follow the maintenance schedule in your service manual.

▶ Change your oil according to the schedule recommended in your service manual and check your oil regularly, perhaps on the first of each month. You may also want to carry an extra quart of oil in your vehicle.

✓ Check your radiator regularly, perhaps on the first of each month, for proper levels of coolant/antifreeze. Consider carrying an extra gallon in the trunk.

✓ Also check the battery monthly to make sure it's adequately charged and maintained.

✓ A significant change in temperature can affect the air in your tires. Check your tires regularly for air pressure and for wear.

▶ Change your windshield wiper blades at the first sign of wear. New blades are relatively inexpensive.

▶ Always be aware of your gas gauge. Know how much gas remains in your tank and the approximate number of miles your car gets per gallon.

▶ Warm up your car before you begin driving. In the winter, doing so will allow time for the windows to defrost. At any time, it will increase the life of your engine.

88. EQUIPPING FOR SAFETY

Outfit your car for safety.

We love our cars and the freedom they represent. Whatever the make and model, they are our main mode of transportation, our transport to dreams, our ticket to ride. They give us the access we crave to the open road. Usually, all they need in return is simple maintenance. Beyond that, for safety's sake, there are a few items that belong in every car.

- Maps get us where we need to go. Carry the appropriate ones no matter how familiar you think you are with the lay of the land.

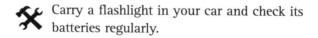 Carry a flashlight in your car and check its batteries regularly.

- Keep a Swiss Army knife in your car. You'll be surprised at how often you'll use it.

- Carry at least one bottle of water—you might need it for drinking *or* for the radiator.

- During the winter, keep a blanket handy.

- Keep an extra pair of sunglasses in your glove box. On bright mornings or afternoons, they could keep you from rear-ending someone.

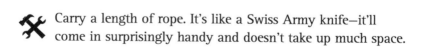 Carry a length of rope. It's like a Swiss Army knife—it'll come in surprisingly handy and doesn't take up much space.

- Don't forget jumper cables, a properly inflated spare tire and tire jack, and a first aid kit.

8 9 . M A P S A N D R O U T E S

Make sure you know where you are going.

Another one of our favorite police officers loves to quote a familiar saying: "If you don't know where you're going, any road will get you there." On the road, as with other facets of your life, uncertainty breeds confusion, and confusion increases your risk of harm. It's far better to plan and prepare before you hit the road, whether for business or pleasure, than to get lost, be lost, and stay lost.

- Most states and many auto clubs offer maps at little or no cost. Use them.

- Several search engines on the Internet now offer "map it" or "drive it" directions. All you need to do is enter your current location and the address of your destination and you will get printed directions and a map to aid your travels.

✓ Check the weather forecast to make sure you aren't driving into a storm or other weather-related circumstance without advance notice.

Keep your radio tuned to a local station so you can follow any unforeseen events along the route.

- Consider the time of day, your schedule, and rush hours as you plan your route.

☎ Call the highway department to check on road conditions.

- Keep change in your car in case you must travel a toll road.

90. REST AREAS

Avoid rest areas
that are isolated and
have little traffic.

As with many safety risks, women are usually more tuned in to the environment at rest areas than men. But such areas pose varying threats for all of us depending on the way they are designed, the time of day, the amount of traffic there, and the personnel assigned to them. A few simple precautions can make the difference between rest and risk.

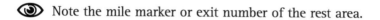 Note the mile marker or exit number of the rest area.

- Keep your doors locked as you drive into the parking area. Note any cars, trucks, or individuals that seem suspicious or make you feel uncomfortable.

- Most rest areas post signs indicating employee hours. Look for them.

- Avoid rest areas that appear isolated, especially those that cannot be seen by highway traffic.

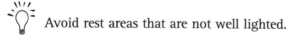 Avoid rest areas that are not well lighted.

- Avoid rest areas that do not have significant vehicular and pedestrian traffic.

- If you feel uncomfortable for any reason when you pull into a rest area, leave at once.

If possible, keep your cell phone turned on and carry it with you when you leave the car.

- If you don't have a cell phone, make note of the location of the pay phone.

- Park as close to the entrance as possible. Lock your car and keep your keys in your hand.

- Do not linger in the area or use it to take a nap.

Ø Do not let young children go into restrooms alone. Do not let them roam out of sight or through the traffic area.

- Leave as quickly as you can.

91. RENTAL CARS

Familiarize yourself with your rental car and the area in which you are traveling.

We both travel quite frequently. One of the things we each like least about travel is rental cars. A rental car usually represents the final leg of a journey. Perhaps you're at the end of a long flight; you're tired; you've stood in line waiting for luggage and then again waiting for the rental car. You're winding down and just want to get where you're going. These are not the best conditions under which to be driving a strange vehicle. Taking precautions on the front end can prevent or reduce risk for the entire journey.

- ► If you are traveling in an unfamiliar area, ask the rental company for a map or for directions.

- ✓ When you first get into the car, take a minute to learn where everything is. Find the lights, the parking brake, the signal indicators, the windshield wipers, even the radio.

- ► When you start the car, make note of the location of the various trouble lights.

- ► Adjust the seat and mirrors before you shift the transmission.

- ► Lock the car.

- 👁 Study the map before you begin driving.

- ► As you drive, note landmarks and mileage markers.

- ► Carry your cell phone with you and keep it turned on.

92. DRIVING DEFENSIVELY

Drive as if your life depended on it.

Bruce was traveling on the interstate recently when he noticed a woman in the adjacent lane eating a hamburger, talking on a cell phone, and checking out her make-up in the mirror—all while driving. She didn't appear to be completing any of the tasks particularly well and wasn't paying much attention to traffic. It takes just a split second for tragedy to occur and she was an accident waiting to happen.

- Maintaining control of your vehicle should be your primary concern when you are behind the wheel.

⊘ Don't pull down the vanity mirror or use the rearview mirror to shave or apply makeup while your car is in motion.

⊘ Don't read the newspaper, correspondence, or anything else as you drive.

- Avoid eating behind the wheel.

- Keep your foot on or very near the gas and brake pedals, even if you engage the cruise-control mechanism.

- Don't steer with your fingertips or your knees.

⊘ Don't turn around to talk to people next to you or in the back seat.

- Cell phones deserve special attention. Whenever possible, pull off the road to talk on the phone. Avoid stressful conversations while you are at the wheel.

Know what to do when your car breaks down.

If something does go wrong with your car while you are on the road, several actions can minimize your danger. Most important, do your best to prevent the situation in the first place by maintaining your vehicle. But if the unavoidable happens, be prepared.

- ▸ It may sound rather simplistic, but know where you are. Keep track of mileage markers so you can communicate your location as specifically as possible.

- ▸ Pull as far off the road as possible and turn on your hazard lights.

 If you have a car phone, use it at once to call the state police, the highway patrol, or the local police.

- ▸ Call a family member or friend to let him know your situation.

- ▸ Call your automobile club or association for assistance.

- ▸ If your vehicle is sufficiently removed from traffic, stay inside the car until assistance arrives.

Ø Don't accept a ride with a stranger.

- ▸ If someone comes along in an unmarked car and claims to be a police officer, ask to see a badge with a name. Ask him to radio for a marked unit to respond.

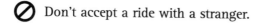

94. RULES OF THE ROAD

Follow your instincts and don't take undue chances.

Last summer's slaying of a woman and two teenage girls in Yosemite reminded us once again how even places that seem safe—that *should be* safe—are not always safe. When you are on the road, remember the very basic rules we all know and should follow. If you decide to be a Good Samaritan and help someone in distress, do so with caution.

- Don't pick up hitchhikers, no matter if they are male or female, young or old. The risk is too great.

⊘ Don't let your children "catch a ride" with a stranger for any reason.

- If you see someone whose car is broken down on the side of the road, stop and offer to make a phone call, but talk to them through a barely opened window. Don't get out to help unless you feel completely comfortable or the situation demands your action.

If you see anyone in trouble and you can't stop, call the state police or highway patrol and report the incident and location.

- If someone follows you or tries to motion you over to the side of the road, don't stop. Drive to the nearest exit and pull into a gas station or restaurant parking lot where other people are close by.

- Watch for posted highway emergency telephone numbers.

95. GETTING YOUR BEARINGS

As you travel, become as familiar as possible with your new environment.

Years ago, a former colleague and safety specialist said something that is as true today as it was then: "Uncertainty breeds confusion and confusion increases risk." Most of us have traveled to an unfamiliar city to attend a conference or event. We check into a hotel in an area we know little about. Criminals know this and are waiting to take advantage of our uncertainty. None of us should be afraid to explore or pursue a thirst for adventure, but we should be mindful of the safety challenges that might be presented.

➤ As you travel, familiarize yourself with the route, looking for landmarks and street signs along the way.

➤ Make it a habit to note mileage.

When you first arrive in an unfamiliar location, examine neighboring buildings for distinguishing characteristics so you can use them as landmarks.

➤ If possible, get out and about during daylight to get your bearings.

➤ Take note of the neighborhood. Is it primarily commercial? Is the area isolated? Does it appear safe? Are restaurants, theaters, or other such spots present in close proximity?

✓ Ask someone—a desk clerk, a police officer, a waitress— about the general safety of the area.

➤ Learn as much as possible so you can act accordingly.

96. FILING A TRAVEL PLAN

When you travel, always let someone else know where you are.

Sometimes the pressures of everyday life get to us and we'd like to get away from everything and everybody—to escape without reporting to a soul. Unfortunately, that's not a particularly safe practice. One of our favorite detectives is fond of saying, "Everybody's got to be somewhere." It is important to let someone else know where your "somewhere" is.

When you travel, let a family member, friend, or colleague know your itinerary, including your general time of departure, your mode of transportation, the route you are traveling, and your expected return time.

► When you arrive at your destination, make contact with someone there so at least one person has seen your face.

Also let your family, friend, or colleague know that you've arrived safe and sound.

► If your plans change, let someone know.

► If you happen to be in an area when an emergency occurs (e.g., a fire, a hurricane), let your contact know you are safe so your loved ones don't worry unduly about you.

✓ Make it a habit to check in with someone at least once a day. That way, if something unforeseen happens, at least one other person will know.

► Keep emergency contact information on your person the entire time you are traveling.

97. WEATHER-PROOFING
YOUR TRAVEL PLANS

Be prepared for anything
nature throws at you.

We both love weather—all kinds of weather, all seasons. We each have been known to drive for hours in the middle of the night to watch a storm pound the coast or to see the season's first snow hit the top of a mountain range. While some may question our sanity, experience has taught us that much of nature's fury can be dealt with, even enjoyed, with proper preparation and a healthy dose of common sense. You've got to know when it's time to "fold 'em" and head for cover.

✓ Before you head out, whether for an hour or a week, get the best, most up-to-date weather information you can. Plan for the forecast. Meteorologists aren't always right, but they have more sophisticated equipment than ever before, and they know more than we do about what may happen. Pay attention to what they say.

- ► Outfit yourself for extremes. Chances are the temperature won't reach record highs or lows, and the storm of the century proba-bly won't hit, but if you are prepared for the worst, the middle range won't ruin your trip.

- ► Carry sufficient emergency provisions—food, water, clothing, sleeping gear—to allow you and your travel companions to spend two nights out if you become stranded due to weather or car trouble.

Be certain your vehicle is well equipped. Extreme heat calls for a container of coolant in the trunk and a complete check of hoses and belts before you leave. For cold-weather excursions take along gear to deal with snow and ice: a window scraper, small shovel, tow rope, tire chains, and some type of throw-down abrasive such as sand or kitty litter.

- Be sensible. Don't exceed the limits of your vehicle or its passengers.

98. HOTELS AND MOTELS

Remember that in hotels you are surrounded by strangers, and act accordingly.

Hotels are a wonderful convenience. They can serve as a vacation host, a business center, or a temporary shelter. But no matter what they want us to believe, a hotel is not really a home away from home. At home you probably aren't sleeping next door to people you've never seen before, and you don't have strangers cleaning your room every day. Use hotels for the amenities they offer, but remember to exercise caution.

- ▶ Almost all hotels post signs telling you not to leave valuables in your room. They do it for a reason: because the risk of loss is significant. Take their advice. Use a room-safe for valuables if one is available, or check with the front desk about a hotel safe.

- ⊘ Do not leave your valuables in your car. Hotel parking lots are a prime target for thieves who know how to work them.

- ▶ Keep your room door locked at all times, even when you are just running down the hall for ice.

- ▶ If there is a door that adjoins your room to the next room, make sure it stays locked.

- ▶ Leave your television or radio on all the time when you are out of the room.

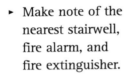 Make note of the evacuation route posted in the room. The next time you leave the room, take that route so you are familiar with it.

- Make note of the nearest stairwell, fire alarm, and fire extinguisher.

✓ When you first check in, count the number of doors in the hallway between your room and the closest emergency exit, and remember the number. If smoke from a fire inhibits your vision but it's still safe to leave your room, you can reach the exit by feel.

- No matter what time of day or night, always evacuate if the fire alarm sounds. Don't assume that the alarm is false and don't worry about personal possessions. In the event of a fire, they can be replaced.

- Check to see if your window is open.

- Make note of the telephone numbers of the hotel operator, the front desk, and security.

- As you walk through the hotel, draw a mental floor plan of the building.

- Park as close to the entrance as possible.

- If your room opens to the outdoors, park as close to your room as possible.

 Park in a well-lit area and keep your car locked.

99. SUBWAYS AND
PUBLIC TRANSPORT

Practice safety strategies
in subways and metros.

One of the safest places in Washington, D.C., is the Metro system, partly because safety figured prominently in its design. Whether you are traveling in Washington or New York, Atlanta or Boston, a subway or metro system can provide a quick route through a heavily trafficked area. A few key behaviors will ensure your safety as well as your arrival.

► Always be aware of your surroundings and your fellow travelers.

► By virtue of their convenience, subways attract large crowds. Keep your purse or your wallet close to your body, where it cannot easily be stolen.

► Unless you know exactly where you are going, take the time to study the map or ask an attendant for directions.

⊘ Do not let your children stand too close to the edge of the platform to "see the train coming."

► Do not let your children out of your sight, even once you are in the car.

► If possible, get a seat. If not, hold onto a safety rail or strap.

 When you arrive at your stop, hold your youngsters' hands when disembarking.

▸ Avoid an isolated stop late at night, or anytime you don't feel comfortable.

100. AIRPORTS

Stay alert to risks in airports.

You have a far greater chance of experiencing serious injury in an automobile than you do in an airplane, but there are still risks associated with air travel. Most of them, unfortunately, involve criminals who are looking for easy targets. Don't let yourself become one.

▸ Airport parking can be a nightmare. Park as close to the terminal as possible.

▸ If you have to park in a deck or garage, park as close to the exit or elevator as you can.

▸ If you use satellite parking, park close to the shuttle stop.

🔅 Park under a light and write down the location of your car. You'd be surprised how quickly you can forget that information.

▸ Keep your luggage in sight at all times.

When you place your personal items on the conveyor belt at the metal detector, wait until they have moved into the view of the camera before you walk through the metal detector. Otherwise, someone can pick up your purse or your laptop and simply melt into the crowd.

- If you use the restroom, do not leave your carry-on luggage on the counter or immediately below the door stall. It's too easy a target for a thief.

- Don't leave your carry-on luggage at the gate, even if you are merely going to the restroom or you want to grab a quick cup of coffee. While you are getting your coffee, someone else could be grabbing your possessions.

101. BUSES AND TRAINS

Be aware of risks on buses and trains.

The romance of train travel seems to have returned as trains enjoy a resurgence in popularity. We live just a couple of hours from Washington, D.C., and often take the train when we travel there. Trains are convenient and safe. The same is true with bus travel. It, too, remains popular, especially bus tours designed for retirees. The precautions you should observe are similar for both.

- Purchase your ticket in advance to avoid carrying and displaying large amounts of cash at the ticket window.

✓ Consider making your reservations or buying your ticket over the Internet. That gives you the opportunity to study the routes available, the accommodations, and the options you have.

- If overhead storage is available on the train or bus, use it, but remember, it is not secure.

- Avoid carrying valuables, such as expensive jewelry.

👁 Note the emergency exits when you board.

- Maintain a general awareness of where you are, the time of day, and weather conditions.

- If emergency information is available, take the time to read it.

wrapping it up

The suggestions and considerations we have offered in these pages are based upon our years of experience. *Keep Safe!,* while broad-based in its attempts to address the most common aspects of modern life, is not intended to be all-encompassing or exclusive. We don't claim to have all the answers for all people and problems. We know we have not exhausted the subject, and we urge you to consult other reference material for more in-depth consideration of many important topics. Our hope is that we have presented at least a few practices everyone will find worth pursuing. We also hope we have prompted you to reframe your thinking and ask yourself new questions—to become more safety conscious overall. One measure of our success will be if the book inspires you to come up with safety tips we haven't mentioned.

As we said in the introduction, we firmly believe the primary role of government is the protection of its people. But no one cares as much about your family's safety and protection as you do. If you're like us, keeping your family safe will always be your principal goal.

We believe it is critical that all of us become more proactive in dealing with safety issues. Whether you are hiking alone on a mountain ridge or fighting your way through rush-hour traffic on the freeway, safety must be a personal concern. As you take more initiative to provide for your well-being and that of your family, your efforts will have a ripple effect. Your model will serve as guidance for others. It is our hope that you will undertake this action as a defined, deliberate objective.

There is no better way to become active in your community than to promote safety. Helping to curb crime, clean up neighborhoods, and reduce the tragic effects of storms and accidents is not just good citizenship; it's good conduct for living. Such time will be well spent.

We have offered a number of ideas and have mentioned several specific programs. Chances are programs exist in your community that we haven't heard of, established and operated by unsung local heroes. Uncertainties abound in the business of providing public safety, but after more than forty years collectively, both of us are absolutely convinced of one premise: crime and safety are intensely local problems, and the very best solutions are local in nature and application. Common sense cannot be legislated; nor can total safety, security, and well-being.

We hope that with our efforts and yours, more of our neighbors, friends, and colleagues will accept the challenge of today's society. With our freedom comes much responsibility. High on the list of those obligations is the duty to avoid doing harm—to ourselves and others.

We chose to deliver our message directly to you because you are the one who will make a real difference. If something you take from this book keeps you, or someone close to you, out of harm's way, then we will know success.

Think safe, act safe, be safe.

For More Information...

For more information about the authors, please consult their website, www.wellsmorris.com.

For additional *Keep Safe!* information, to learn about additional *Keep Safe!* projects, or to submit your safety tip or story, contact www.tokeepsafe.com.

Hunter House
SMART FUN SERIES

101 MUSIC GAMES FOR CHILDREN: Fun and Learning with Rhythm and Song by Jerry Storms

For playing with children ages four and up. The games in 101 MUSIC GAMES help to develop listening and trust, concentration and improvisation, and group interaction and expression. All you need to play are music tapes or CDs and simple instruments, many of which kids can have fun making from common household items. Many games are especially good for large group settings such as birthday parties and day care. Others are easily adapted to meet classroom needs. More than 200,000 copies sold in 12 languages worldwide.

160 pages ... 30 illus. ... Paperback $11.95 ... Spiral bound $14.95

101 DANCE GAMES FOR CHILDREN by Paul Rooyackers

For playing with children ages four and up. The games in 101 DANCE GAMES help to develop self-esteem, physical coordination, and sociability and relaxation techniques. Guided by the understanding that the body has a special language of its own, this book encourages children to interact and express how they feel in creative fantasies— without words. Charmingly illustrated, the dance games in this book combine movement and play in ways that release children's spontaneity and promote confident self-expression. They are organized into meeting and greeting games, cooperation games, story dances, party dances, "muscle puzzles," dances with props, and more.

160 pages ... 30 illus. ... Paperback $11.95 ... Spiral bound $14.95

101 DRAMA GAMES FOR CHILDREN: Fun and Learning with Acting and Make-Believe by Paul Rooyackers

For playing with children ages four and up. The "play-ful" ideas in 101 DRAMA GAMES help to develop creativity and improvisation, communication and trust, self-esteem and personality. These noncompetitive games include: introduction games, sensory games, pantomime games, story games, sound games, games with masks, games with costumes, and many more. Each drama game contains an age guideline, an estimated time of play, and suggestions for the most appropriate type of music. The games can be played by children and adults of all ages, and are flexible enough to be used by parents, teachers, camp leaders, daycare providers, or other group leaders in a variety of settings.

160 pages ... 30 illus. ... Paperback $11.95 ... Spiral bound $14.95

To order books see last page or call (800) 266-5592

ORDER FORM

10% DISCOUNT on orders of $50 or more —
20% DISCOUNT on orders of $150 or more —
30% DISCOUNT on orders of $500 or more —
On cost of books for fully prepaid orders

NAME

ADDRESS

CITY/STATE   ZIP/POSTCODE

PHONE   COUNTRY (outside of U.S.)

TITLE	QTY	PRICE	TOTAL
Keep Safe! (paperback)		@ $12.95	
		@	

Prices subject to change without notice

Please list other titles below:

		@ $	
		@ $	
		@ $	
		@ $	
		@ $	
		@ $	
		@ $	

Check here to receive our book catalog ☐   FREE

Shipping Costs:
First book: $3.00 by book post ($4.50 by UPS, Priority Mail, or to ship outside the U.S.)
Each additional book: $1.00
For rush orders and bulk shipments call us at (800) 266-5592

TOTAL	_____
Less discount @_____%	(_____)
TOTAL COST OF BOOKS	_____
Calif. residents add sales tax	_____
Shipping & handling	_____
TOTAL ENCLOSED	_____

Please pay in U.S. funds only

☐ Check ☐ Money Order ☐ Visa ☐ Mastercard ☐ Discover

Card # _____ Exp. date _____

Signature _____

Complete and mail to:
Hunter House Inc., Publishers
PO Box 2914, Alameda CA 94501-0914
Orders: (800) 266-5592   email: ordering@hunterhouse.com
Phone (510) 865-5282 Fax (510) 865-4295
☐ Check here to receive our book catalog

KSF 3/00